NEW ZEALAND FROM THE AIR

CRAIG POTTON

CRAIG POTTON PUBLISHING &
HODDER MOA BECKETT PUBLISHERS

DEDICATION

This book is dedicated to Alex, Paul and Peter, who love to
fly, but most of all to my father, who made the book possible
and gave me every encouragement.

Published by: Craig Potton Publishing Ltd, 98 Vickerman Street,
            PO Box 555, Nelson, New Zealand,
            and
            Hodder Moa Beckett Publishers Limited, 28 Poland Road, Glenfield,
            PO Box 100-749, NSMC, Auckland 1330, New Zealand

Photography: Craig Potton
Text: Annie Wheeler and Craig Potton
Publishing Coordinator: Robbie Burton
Cover Design: Jo Williams Design
Design: Donna Hoyle
Filmwork: Peter Dorn, Printgroup, Wellington
Colour Separations: Rob MacCleod, Lithographic Laboratory, Wellington
Typeset by Jazz Graphics
Printed through Bookbuilders, Hong Kong

First published 1992 as 'Above New Zealand'
Revised and updated 1995

© Copyright: Craig Potton Publishing and Hodder Moa Beckett Publishers

© Copyright photographs: Craig Potton

ISBN 0-908802-27-7
ISBN 0-908802-11-0 (Above New Zealand)

PAGES 2 & 3: Farmland along the Tukituki
River, south of Hastings, Hawke's Bay.

PAGE 4: Sunrise on the northern slopes of
Mt Cook, Mount Cook National Park.

PAGE 5: Dawn on the summits of Mts
Ngauruhoe (foreground) and Ruapehu,
Tongariro National Park.

PAGES 6 & 7: Gullied volcanic ash and
steaming fumaroles, White Island,
Bay of Plenty.

CONTENTS

Introduction

IHAVE ALWAYS wanted to climb high and then look back down to where I've come from. When we were young my friends and I built tree huts and spent hours viewing a world below us that was almost comic in its detached distance. Dogs would bark, mothers would shout and everyone seemed to trot about in circles that little affected us.

Years later I and some of those same friends started climbing mountains. I climbed for the view beyond and below. Seen from a high peak, the world is sublimely beautiful, but it is also detached, and climbing is a dangerous game. There is a very real limit to how long I want to spend on any summit before returning to the comfort and conviviality of the lowlands and the warmth of life below the bushline. However, after every return, I think of going high again.

When I look down from a helicopter onto places and landscapes I love, it is a radically different experience. I sit suspended in a vast blue sky, feeling as if I am somewhere between nothing and everything. Above me is infinite space and below me a huge warm land bordered by the enfolding sea. Light seems to caress the earth, softly melding colours with colours, warmth with cold, positive with negative. These are the images that I reach out to compose with my camera. From this height patterns are much more obvious than they are from ground level, or from trees, or from mountain peaks. The higher I rise the bigger the picture becomes and the underlying folds and forms of the natural landscape and works of people take on more and more apparent order.

Although, like Icarus, I delight in simply flying free from the weight of gravity, I am also enchanted by encountering more ordered views of the world. Yet I remain ambivalent about the insights that flight has given me and, like Daedalus, I am fearful that I have overstepped some natural boundary. The images in this book may be Olympian in their detachment from the personal rounds of our daily life, but is this impersonal perspective a strength or a weakness?

All I can really express is the hope that these photographs have managed to provide images of a world imbued with a more overt form than is usually apparent and that, if form implies purposefulness and meaning, this is a significant insight. And if the earth's structure is laid beautifully bare by distance, I hope it will help us to reflect on how fragile, and at times how foolish, our connections to the earth really are.

CRAIG POTTON

The lower reaches of the Clarence River, in the Inland
Kaikoura Range.

OPPOSITE: The mouth of the Makawhio (or Jacobs) River in South Westland, with Mt Tasman and Mt Cook on the distant skyline.

CHAPTER 1
The West Coast

Sunset on Mt Tasman.

HEMMED IN between the stormy expanse of the Tasman Sea and the seemingly impenetrable barrier of the Southern Alps, the West Coast of the South Island is a land apart. For 600 km from the Karamea district in the north to the Cascade River in the south this wild and often sparsely populated region overwhelms visitors with its natural beauty — mountains and glaciers, tranquil lakes and unruly rivers, forests draped in mosses and ferns, and a wild coastline. As for the inhabitants, no other region of New Zealand has achieved quite the same celebrity or degree of individuality that attaches to "The Coast", and nowhere else does the pioneer past remain as close

13

to the surface of contemporary life.

While there is certainly no shortage of magnificent scenery on the West Coast, what really distinguishes this part of the country is the extent to which the region has managed to remain in its natural condition, even in the neighbourhood of its main areas of settlement. Only on the West Coast does nature's scheme remain widely in evidence, with dense forest still covering much of the land between the mountains and the sea, and substantial areas of wetland patchworking the coastal plains, especially in the south. To put this aspect of the West Coast in perspective we perhaps need to remember that over 90% of New Zealand's natural wetlands have been drained and reclaimed since human settlement, and over 80% of its lowland forests have been felled to make way for pasture or exotic plantations. Thus, for example, the 40,000 ha of kahikatea forest that today lines much of the highway through South Westland is, in terms of the country as a whole, merely the last 2% of a type of forest that once covered much of the fertile lowlands throughout New Zealand.

Coasters are proud of both their isolation and their ability to coexist with the wild, primeval landscape on their doorstep. Making a living from this part of the country has never been easy. The extraction of greenstone, gold, timber and coal from the West Coast's rugged terrain have all provided important chapters in New Zealand's social history, as have the often herculean efforts involved in constructing road and rail links into this natural fortress. A series of major gold rushes in the mid-1860s saw the West Coast population explode within the space of a year or so from a few hundred to upwards of 30,000.

Although gold was the lure that drew people across the Southern Alps, coal was the commodity that kept them there. Great seams of "black gold" in the southern Paparoa Range and on the Buller plateau saw Greymouth and Westport develop into sizeable ports, a transalpine railway constructed over Arthur's Pass, and the beginnings of the New Zealand Labour Party in the mining unions formed in West Coast coal towns such as Denniston, Runanga and Blackball. Today the traditional West Coast extractive industries have all been overtaken by tourism, which West Coasters are gradually coming to accept as the best sustainable use of the vast natural resources of the region.

No introduction to the West Coast would be complete without mention of its weather statistics, especially the legendary rainfall. Large volumes of rain do bucket down on the region from time to time, although the amount varies considerably. Westport receives "only" about 2000 mm annually, Haast nearer 3000 mm, Fox Glacier and Franz Josef 5000 mm, and probably upwards of 10,000 mm falls in some of the mountain valleys of South Westland. It sounds a lot and, indeed, it is. Among endless examples of what can result from the more destructive storms are the two catastrophic floods suffered by Greymouth during the 1980s, and the washing away of the Gates of Haast bridge twice within the space of a few years of the opening of the Haast Pass Highway in 1960. But to bring some balance to these rather daunting rainfall statistics it needs to be added that many of the settled parts of the West Coast also enjoy a surprisingly generous quota of sunshine — about 1800 hours a year (an average of five hours a day) at Fox Glacier and Franz Josef, and a balmy 2000 hours at Westport and Karamea.

It is also worth bearing in mind that much of the scenery and natural drama for which the West Coast is famous depends ultimately on an ample supply of rain. It is, after all, this much maligned rain that nourishes the forests and wetlands, sends rivers and streams cascading over waterfalls and tumbling out of mountain valleys, and restocks the high ice reservoirs, allowing glaciers to trespass further into the accessible lowlands than they do anywhere else in the world at comparable latitudes.

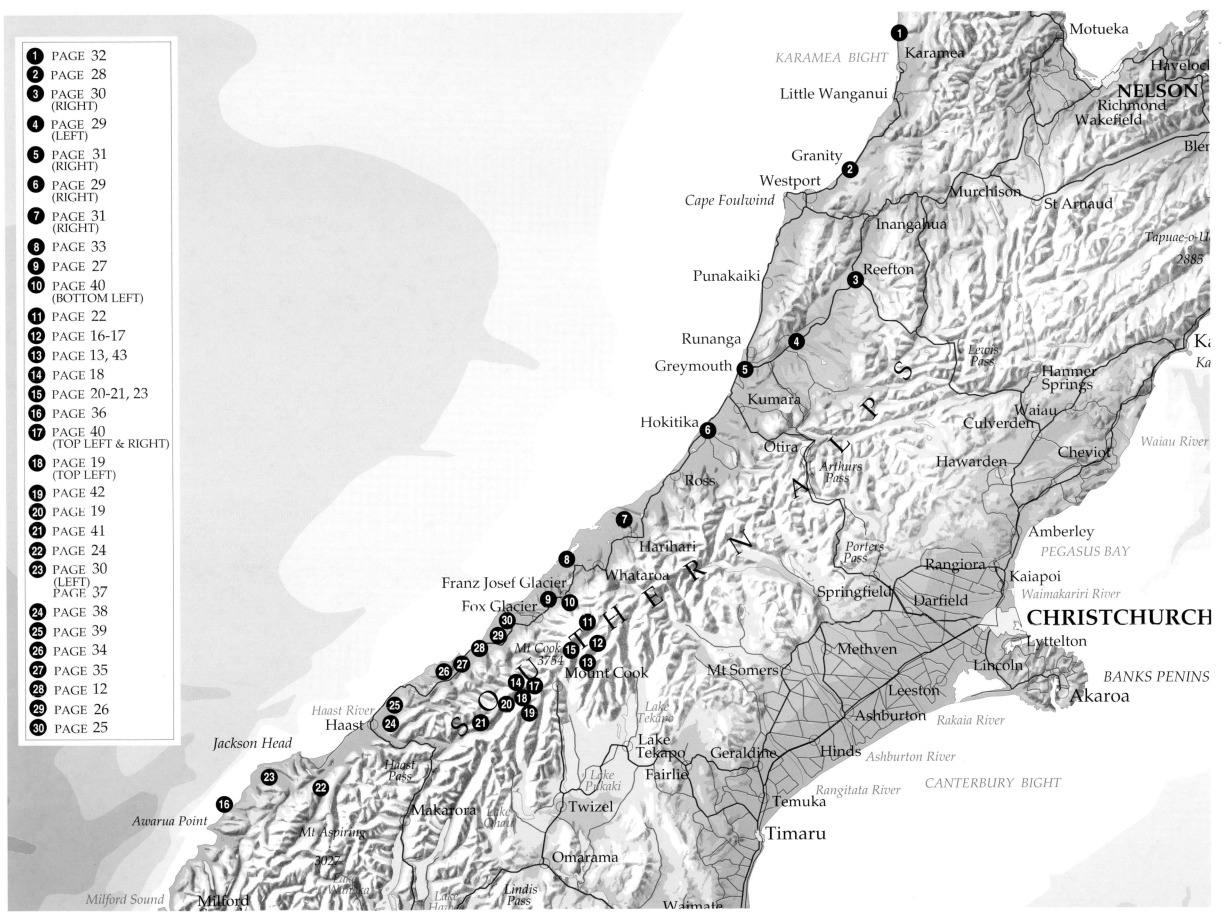

Motueka

KARAMEA BIGHT Karamea

Little Wanganui

Havelock

NELSON
Richmond
Wakefield

Granity

Westport

Bler

Cape Foulwind

Murchison   St Arnaud

Inangahua

Tapuae-o-U
2885

Punakaiki

Reefton

Ka
Ka

Runanga

Lewis Pass

Greymouth

Hanmer Springs

Kumara

Waiau

Culverden

Waiau River

Hokitika

Otira

Hawarden

Cheviot

Ross

Arthurs Pass

Harihari

Porters Pass

Amberley

PEGASUS BAY

Whataroa

Rangiora

Kaiapoi

Franz Josef Glacier

Springfield

Darfield

Waimakariri River

Fox Glacier

CHRISTCHURCH

Mt Cook 3754

Lyttelton

Mount Cook

Methven

Lincoln

Mt Somers

BANKS PENINS

Akaroa

Leeston

Haast River

Ashburton

Haast

Lake Tekapo

Hinds

Ashburton River

Rakaia River

Jackson Head

Haast Pass

Lake Tekapo

Geraldine

Rangitata River

CANTERBURY BIGHT

Lake Pukaki

Fairlie

Temuka

Awarua Point

Makarora

Lake Ohau

Twizel

Timaru

Mt Aspiring 3027

Omarama

Waimate

Milford Sound Milford

Lindis Pass

15

Sunset on the névé of the Fox Glacier. Both photographs are taken from
virtually the same position, the one to the left looking south towards the ice
summit of Mt Tasman (3498 m) while the other turns through 180 degrees to
take in the western flanks of the Fritz Range and the distant Tasman Sea.

A closer view of the southwest flank of Mt Sefton
(3157 m) and the Douglas Névé.

ABOVE: The head of the Landsborough River with the summit ridge of Mt Cook flanked by Mt Tasman (left) and Mt Sefton in the far distance. The Landsborough flows parallel to the Main Divide for 60 km before joining the Haast River for its final 45 km to the sea. During the Ice Ages the longest glacier in the Southern Alps issued from these valleys to about 20 km beyond the present coastline.

RIGHT: Ice-steepened schist faces near Mt Dechen on the Hooker Range, west of the Landsborough River.

OVERLEAF: The high icefields at the head of the Fox Glacier merge above the main icefall.

ABOVE: Precipitation that can often exceed 10,000 mm a year dumps so much snow on the mountains of Westland National Park that the icefalls of the Franz Josef (LEFT) and Fox Glaciers continue to trespass well down into the lowlands.

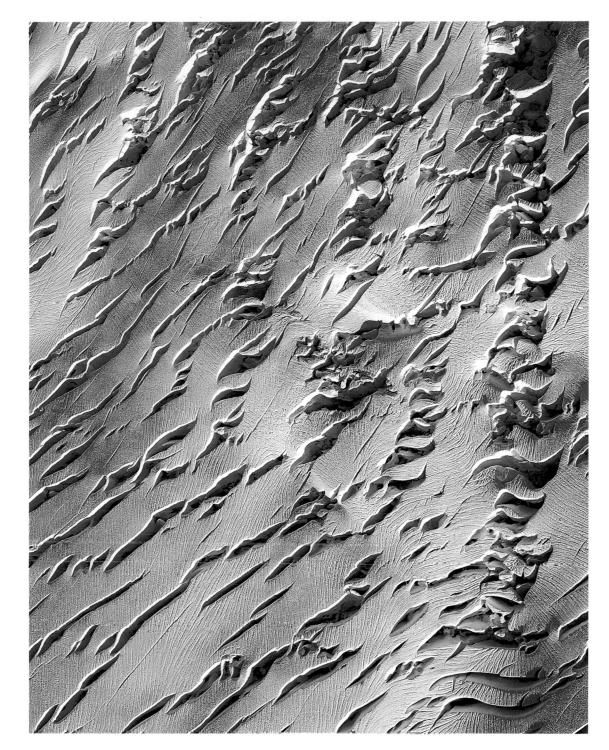

RIGHT: In the steepest sections of their icefalls, these glaciers advance as rapidly as 5–6 m a day, putting them amongst the fastest glaciers in the world, and resulting in a confused jumble of pressure ridges, seracs and crevasses.

OPPOSITE: Midway on its long journey northwards from the Barrier and Olivine Ranges to the sea at Jackson Bay, the Arawata River is joined by the Waipara River, which drains the Bonar Glacier on the southwest flanks of Mt Aspiring (3027 m).

Once clear of the confines of their mountain valleys, the Fox and Cook Rivers join together to cross the broad flat glacial outwash plain below the village of Fox Glacier.

OPPOSITE: Dense kahikatea forest cloaks the banks of the Ohinetamatea (or Saltwater) River as it winds across the coastal lowlands south of the Cook River. Forest like this was once widespread in lowland New Zealand, but is now virtually confined to South Westland.

Pasture on the broad flats of the Waiho River near Franz Josef, dotted with remnant clumps of a once extensive totara forest.

OPPOSITE: The huge open-cast coal mine at Stockton, north of Westport.

A vertical perspective reveals old river channels in this pastoral land in the broad valley of the Grey River.

As much a repository of the region's history as the museum, Hokitika's orderly cemetery occupies a terrace overlooking the northern part of the town and the Tasman Sea.

LEFT: At the roadend south of Haast the Cascade River wends its way seawards in a sequence of classic meanders, "the only river in South Westland that is in no hurry to reach the sea", according to the great West Coast explorer Charles Douglas.

From 1870 Reefton was the main quartz-crushing centre of the West Coast goldfields, and in 1888 it became the first town in the Southern Hemisphere to be lit by electricity.

Greymouth is both the largest West Coast town (pop. 8000) and the most precariously sited. Twice during the 1980s catastrophic floods have inundated the central business district and low-lying suburbs south of the river.

RIGHT: The lower reaches of the Whanganui River. Typical of the coastal lowlands west of the Southern Alps, farmland is mostly confined to the river flats, while the hills — which are almost invariably old lateral moraines deposited by Ice Age glaciers — remain forested.

OPPOSITE: The mouth of the Heaphy River, 15 km beyond the end of the road north of Karamea. The Heaphy Track, a popular tramping route linking the Karamea region with Golden Bay, can be seen briefly on the southern bank of the river.

Stained by tannins and humus from the surrounding forest, a stream wends its way in leisurely meanders across the bed of the tidal Three Mile Lagoon in Westland National Park.

OPPOSITE: Wilderness beach, lowland forest and freshwater wetlands at Ohinemaka, south of Bruce Bay. During the past 150 years over 90% of New Zealand's freshwater wetlands have been drained and "reclaimed", and only in South Westland are large areas of swampy terrain still widespread.

A dense stand of windshorn rimu forest grows virtually to the brink of the waves at Bruce Bay. In the distance, New Zealand's three highest mountains (Tasman, Dampier and Cook) tower above the intervening ranges.

Patterns created by sand, streams and ocean currents in the wilderness coastline between the Cascade River and Big Bay, at the southern extremity of South Westland.

OPPOSITE: The huge lateral moraine north of the Cascade River ends abruptly in precipitous sea cliffs. Toxic rocks and soils derived from the highly mineralised Red Hills mean that large areas of this sprawling moraine carry only scrub and tussock.

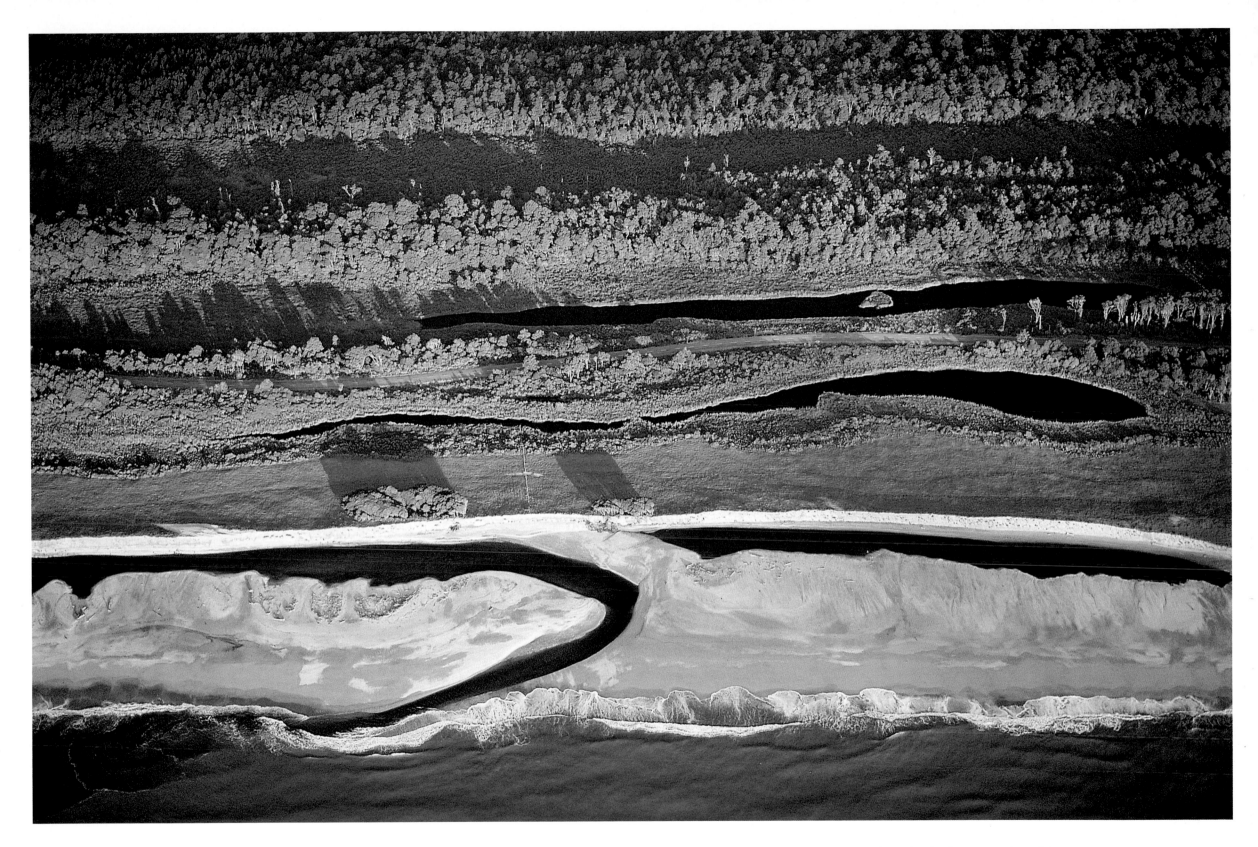

OPPOSITE: Swamp and kahikatea forest beside the Tawharekiri (Maori) Lake on the coastal plain just north of the Haast River.

The mouth of the Waita River, 10 km north of Haast. At the outer edge of the Haast coastal plain there is a unique sequence of parallel dune ridges and impounded lakes, formed by a combination of slow uplift of the land and oscillations in climate and sea levels.

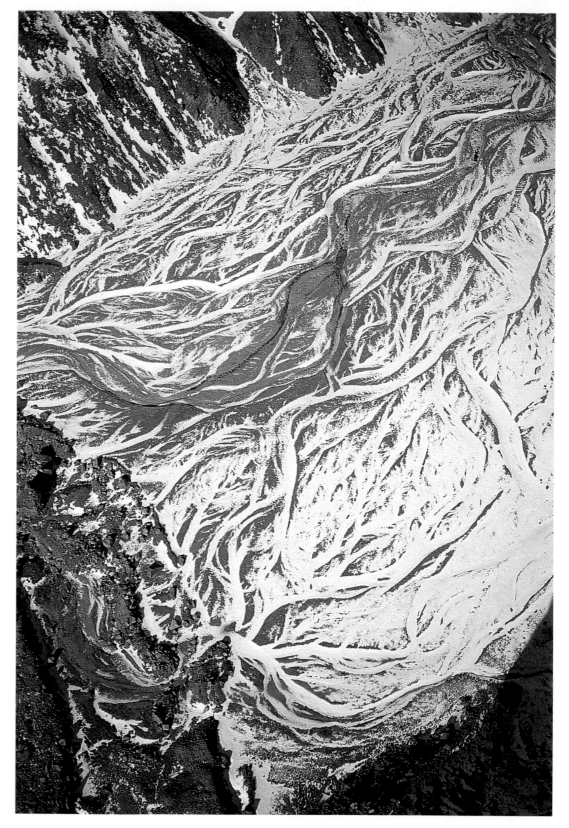

TOP: A small tributary of the Douglas River skirts a large wall of lateral moraine.

Murky with glacial grit, the Waiho River rages between two large schist boulders just below the terminal ice face of the Franz Josef Glacier.

A light snowfall dusts a river flat recently vacated by a shrinking glacier at the head of the Douglas River.
The complex pattern of channels weaving to and fro across the gravels provides an excellent example of the way floodwater streams distribute and level debris left by retreating glaciers.

OPPOSITE: Mt Hooker, north of the Haast Pass, at dusk.

Looking east from near the head of the Landsborough River across jagged summits south of Mt Cook National Park.

OPPOSITE: Moonrise over the north shoulder of Mt Tasman at dusk.

CHAPTER 2
Fiordland, Otago, Southland & Stewart Island

A ridgecrest in the Red Hills Range.

OPPOSITE: The Red Hills, with the snow-capped Olivine Range in the background. Geologists believe that these Red Hills were once close neighbours of very similar mineral-rich ranges found today in Nelson.

THE "deep south" of Fiordland, Otago, Southland and Stewart Island is a region built from several massive blocks of uplifted bedrock that have been sculptured by relentless ice sheets and glaciers. In this southern quarter, the South Island loses the distinctive north–south alignment of the Southern Alps and its adjacent plains, and sprawls to its greatest width in a series of huge, evenly eroded plateaux. Fiordland (composed mainly of New Zealand's most ancient and resilient igneous rock) acts as an immovable barrier, forcing the younger schists to the north into sweeping eastward arcs that extend from Mt Aspiring National Park right through Central Otago to the east coast.

Fiordland beggars the usual superlatives of landscape description. It is huge: the 1.2 million ha of Fiordland National Park is greater than all the other South Island national parks combined. It is wild: rain falls in bucket loads, often exceeding 7 m per year. It has grandeur: resilient 400-million-year-old bedrock has been gouged by giant glaciers leaving steep mountains, brooding lakes and deep U-shaped fiords whose sea walls rise near vertically for upwards of 2000 m.

To the north and east of Fiordland lie the extensive mountain, basin and range landscapes of Otago. These landscapes are almost wholly composed of schist, a rock type that erodes in uneven slabs along distinct planes. There is a large variety of surface expression to the schists of Otago: steep and sheer in the angular peaks and ridges of Mt Aspiring National Park, massive irregular slabs in the Queenstown–Wanaka region, and gently rolling, evenly eroded, high plateaux through much of Central Otago. This last region has been planed smooth by the long action of ice, wind and water into one of New Zealand's most distinctive landscapes. Standing in the rain shadow of the Alps (receiving as little as 350 mm a year), covered in tawny yellow tussocks, and broken by sporadic outcrops of resilient rock obelisks, this Central Otago landscape is starkly beautiful.

The coastal plains and rolling hills of Southland and Otago are not caught in the same rain shadow as Central Otago and receive a good share of the wet southerly weather that flows up the southeastern flanks of New Zealand. This extra moisture feeds the green pastures of Southland and coastal Otago, and the native forest of the remote Catlins Forest Park on the southeast coast. Throughout Southland, and on the lower flats of Otago's Taieri River, highly productive land has been created with extensive swamp drainage and the use of fertilisers to correct imbalances in the post-glacial soils.

Although the climate was obviously a bleak contrast for Maori pioneers used to tropical temperatures, there were two highly prized treasures that attracted significant numbers of Maori south. Firstly, the presence of moa, the giant flightless bird, offered an important food source and a new way of life. However, as the moa were hunted to extinction, and aided over the same period by a significant cooling in the climate and the eruption of tribal wars, Maori numbers were greatly reduced. Inter-tribal fighting was also inevitably tied to access to the second major booty of the deep south — greenstone from the shores of Lake Wakatipu — and by the time Europeans arrived last century, Maori settlement was largely confined to smallish coastal settlements.

The deep south was then settled by a European people well used to the rigours of a tough climate and landscape. Scottish settlers, versed in the work ethic of Calvinism, sailed into Otago Harbour in 1848 and quickly carved out a small colonial enclave. Soon major sheep runs extended throughout the tussocklands of Otago and Southland, and the cities of Dunedin and Invercargill and the towns of Oamaru and Balclutha were built, solid and fortress-like against the elements. This steady progress of land settlement and orderly urban development was explosively interrupted when payable goldfields were discovered in Central Otago in 1861. Townships sprang up throughout Central Otago, as far west as Queenstown, and Dunedin became the largest and richest city in the country. Grand Victorian edifices such as the railway station, Otago University, the cathedral and Larnach's Castle made Dunedin a showcase of successful colonialism.

Otago and Southland have felt the cold hand of economic decline over the last few decades, with the relative prosperity of the north drawing people and industry away. The people of the deep south, though, have strenuously fought against such loss, and Southland's progressive farming and fishing base has encouraged the development of some large industries, such as the aluminium smelter at Bluff. The people of Otago have been equally enterprising in building on the tourist potential of Dunedin's Victorian heritage and the natural values of the Otago Peninsula. However, it is inland, particularly around Queenstown, that the new "gold rush" of tourism has taken off. Originally based on lakeside attractions, famous walks such as the Milford Track, and winter skiing, tourists are now offered an inspiring range of adventure experiences, the most popular of which include jet boating, bungy jumping and white-water rafting.

OVERLEAF: The sculpting hand of Ice Age glaciers remains most pronounced in the hard crystalline rocks of Fiordland, where minimal post-glacial erosion has left a superb sequence of U-shaped valleys (many of them inundated by sea to become fiords), sharp ridges and horn summits, landforms nowhere better displayed than at Milford Sound. Prominent peaks are Mitre Peak (left) and Mt Pembroke (right), the latter still carrying a remnant of the great Milford Glacier that would once have filled this fiord.

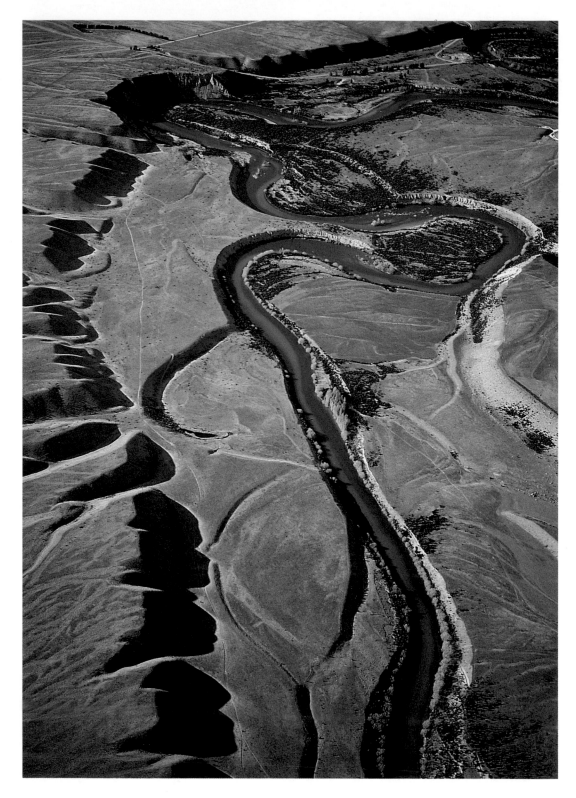

Lake Wanaka, looking
north towards the
Makarora Valley and
the mountains
surrounding the
Haast Pass.

LEFT: Queenstown,
on the shores of Lake
Wakatipu, with The
Remarkables
mountains in the
background.

Textbook examples of river terraces and
meanders in the Clutha River near its origins in
the outlets of Lakes Wanaka and Hawea.

OPPOSITE: Mt Aspiring (3027 m)
and the Bonar Glacier at sunset.
Known to the Maori as Tititea ("the
upright glistening one"), Mt Aspiring
is the only peak in New Zealand
outside the Mt Cook region to exceed
3000 m.

OPPOSITE: Lake Wakatipu between Queenstown and Glenorchy, with the mouth of the Greenstone River on the near side of the lake and the Richardson Mountains in the distance. Pigeon (left) and Pig Islands are roches moutonnées, hard bedrock outcrops that resisted the eroding power of the glacier that carved out the deep groove now occupied by New Zealand's longest lake.

Sheep pasture near Queenstown, towards the end of summer. The seasons are very pronounced in Central Otago, and the Queenstown district is renowned for its magnificent autumn displays.

The lonely lighthouse at Puysegur Point, a headland at the southwestern corner of the South Island, often battered by gale force winds and mountainous seas.

ABOVE: Milford Sound with Mitre Peak in the centre and snow-covered Llawrenny Peaks to the left.

The Sutherland Falls on the Milford Track are the highest in New Zealand (and among the highest in the world), tumbling 580 m from Lake Quill (ABOVE and LEFT) in three continuous leaps.

Scenes from Fiordland's magnificent wilderness coastline.
LEFT: The mouth of the Hollyford River at Martins Bay, north of Milford Sound, with Lake McKerrow filling much of the floor of the lower Hollyford Valley.
ABOVE: Anchor Island at the entrance to Dusky Sound.
OPPOSITE: Exposed open coast near Puysegur Point.

Range after range of craggy Fiordland mountains west of Lake Manapouri.

Lake Iceburg in the headwaters of the North Branch of
the Clinton River.

RIGHT: Streams and rivulets fed by
snowmelt tumble down the sheer
rock walls of the Clinton Valley
beside the Milford Track. Parts of
Fiordland receive over 6000 mm of
rain each year, and in heavier
deluges whole sections of
mountainside become walls of
cascading water.

Most of Stewart Island's 1746 km² is wild, uninhabited country and the only real settlement is at Halfmoon Bay (resident population about 500), on the more sheltered eastern coast.

ABOVE: The Rugged Islands off the northwest corner of the main island.

LEFT: Mason Bay on the windswept west coast.

A colony of blackbrowed mollymawks nesting on volcanic cliffs on Campbell Island, the most southerly of New Zealand's outlying islands.

OPPOSITE: The granite tors of Gog and Magog, near the southern tip of Stewart Island.

Te Waewae Bay, the westernmost farming district on the
Southland coast.

TOP: A small island in Waituna Lagoon, just
south of Invercargill, a "Wetland of
International Importance" for migratory
wading birds.

ABOVE: The port of Bluff with the
Tiwai Point aluminium smelter beyond.

OPPOSITE: The wild, inaccessible and densely
forested southeast coast of Stewart Island.

High tide encircles a sandspit in the Waituna Lagoon, whose rhythmic contours,
fashioned by wind and waves, have been partially disfigured by vehicle tracks.
OPPOSITE: Sheep farming country along the main highway near Lake Te Anau.

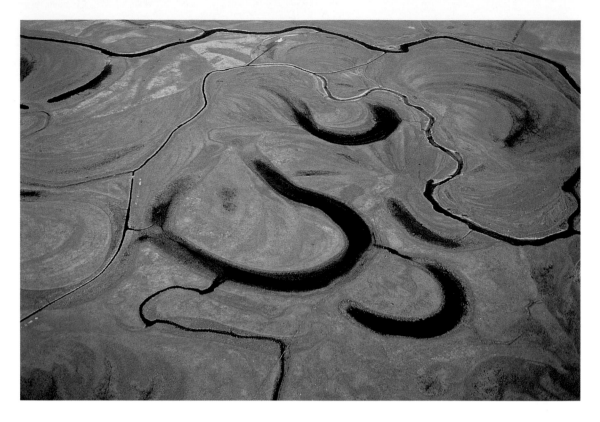

Serpentine meanders are a feature of the Taieri River over much of its 200 km journey from the Lammerlaw Range to the sea south of Dunedin. The two images above show parts of the upper reaches of the river flowing through drained farmland. Just west of the headwaters, Lake Onslow has been formed by damming the nearby Teviot River, and the maze of waterways at the head of the lake (RIGHT and OPPOSITE) shows what the upper reaches of the Taieri would have been like before being converted to farmland.

ABOVE: A winter's morning in the upper Clutha Valley near Lowburn.
OPPOSITE, TOP & RIGHT: Much of inland Otago north of the middle sections of the
Clutha River consists of ranges of flattened hills (Knobby, Lammerlaw and Lammermoor
Ranges) cut by a myriad of stream gullies.

LEFT (top): Dredge tailings on the Earnscleugh Flats across the Clutha River from nearby Alexandra. The fortunes of Alexandra waned after the heyday of the Central Otago goldfields in the 1860s, but were revived in a period of dredging that began in the 1890s and lasted until 1963. Dunedin (below left) pictured here above its distinctive octagonal pattern of streets in the city centre, was the country's richest city during the 1860s goldrush.

ABOVE: Port Chalmers and Otago Harbour with Quarantine Island at the left.

OPPOSITE: Black Head, on the coast south of Dunedin near Waldronville, a promontory comprised of volcanic basalt columns.

Ice overflowing from the Grand Plateau tumbles down the Hochstetter Icefall to join the moraine-covered trunk of the Tasman Glacier, 1150 m below.

OPPOSITE: Morning light softens the east face of Mt Tasman and the Grand Plateau, Mt Cook National Park.

CHAPTER 3
Canterbury

ALTHOUGH THE landscape east of the Southern Alps has been constructed from the same materials and processes as that on the West Coast, and consequently has many parallel landforms (rapidly eroding mountains, glaciers, large outwash plains and braided rivers), few places anywhere in the world show such a complete change of scenery as that which occurs within the space of a few kilometres east and west of the South Island's Southern Alps.

As you move from the West Coast into Canterbury, the rainfall can diminish to as much as a tenth, causing colours to flip from the west's deep forest greens to the yellow hues of tussock grasslands and, further east, to a medley of pastoral greens and golds. In human terms it appears to be an eastward journey in time through the West Coast's pioneering landscape, rough-hewn from an aggressive natural world, into a well-manicured European rural scene in which the original cloak of native forest has all but disappeared.

As if to parallel the west–east transition from apparent disorder to order, the dominant landscape features east of the Alps adhere to a reasonably regular pattern. The crest of the Southern Alps forms a backdrop to the whole of the region, reaching an apex in South Canterbury's Mt Cook National Park, where New Zealand's highest mountains and largest glaciers are clustered together. Running north from here, substantial peaks and glaciers reach as far as Arthur's Pass National Park. Against the Main Divide the lower flanks of the mountains are mostly covered in a uniform canopy of beech forest, although it quickly gives way to the tawny native tussock that covers so much of the Canterbury high country's subsidiary ranges. These foothills to the east of the Alps are broken by huge braided river valleys, a series of inland basins (the biggest being the Mackenzie Basin) and large high-country lakes — Ohau, Tekapo, Pukaki, Coleridge and Sumner.

The big rivers of this region are legendary. Following the paths of old glaciers, rivers such as the Waitaki, Rangitata, Rakaia and Waimakariri have carried massive volumes of glacial debris out beyond the ranges to the coast, to create the Canterbury Plains, the largest area of level terrain in New Zealand.

The other outstanding landscape feature of this part of the country is the old volcanic island of Banks Peninsula, created offshore in a series of major eruptions that ended more than 5 million years ago. Today "the Peninsula" provides two excellent natural deep-water harbours (Lyttelton and Akaroa) in an otherwise harbourless stretch of coastline, and its hills and valleys carry the only real remnants of native forest growing within easy reach of Christchurch.

The Canterbury coast and plains were well populated in early times by Maori, whose hunting and destruction of habitat through uncontrolled burning led to the extinction of the moa. Intriguing rock paintings of moa from this era have survived in dry limestone caverns and overhangs throughout the region.

When the first European settlers arrived at Banks Peninsula they were greeted by a vast arena of treeless plains and swamps. It was land immediately available for agriculture and, although attempts were made to reserve it for weathly gentleman farmers, much was, in fact, better suited to small holdings of mixed cropping and livestock. In the high-country foothills, however, huge sheep runs were established by rich colonists, and today many of these runs are still held by the families that pioneered them.

Sprawling out across the plains to the north and west of Banks Peninsula is the city of Christchurch, frequently described as the most English of New Zealand cities, and by far the largest population centre in the South Island. The Anglican cathedral, gothic and Victorian architecture, large leafy Hagley Park, oak-lined avenues, meandering Avon and Heathcote Rivers, resident monarchist Wizard and winter smogs help preserve something of an English character that was clearly more pervasive in the past, but now tends to be confined to a couple of the wealthier residential areas and those parts of the central city that have managed to survive the recent invasion of tall, square, glass-bound buildings. Much of Christchurch's charm and appeal lies in the balance it seems so often to strike between the old and the new, the traditional and the avant-garde, the artistic and the economic.

Indeed, the future of Canterbury is to a great extent written in its successful past. Wool, meat and crop production are still at the centre of the local economy, although this is increasingly being supplemented by a fast-developing tourist trade that features such attractions as excellent skiing, salmon fishing and even pleasant pastoral settings for the weddings of Japanese tourists.

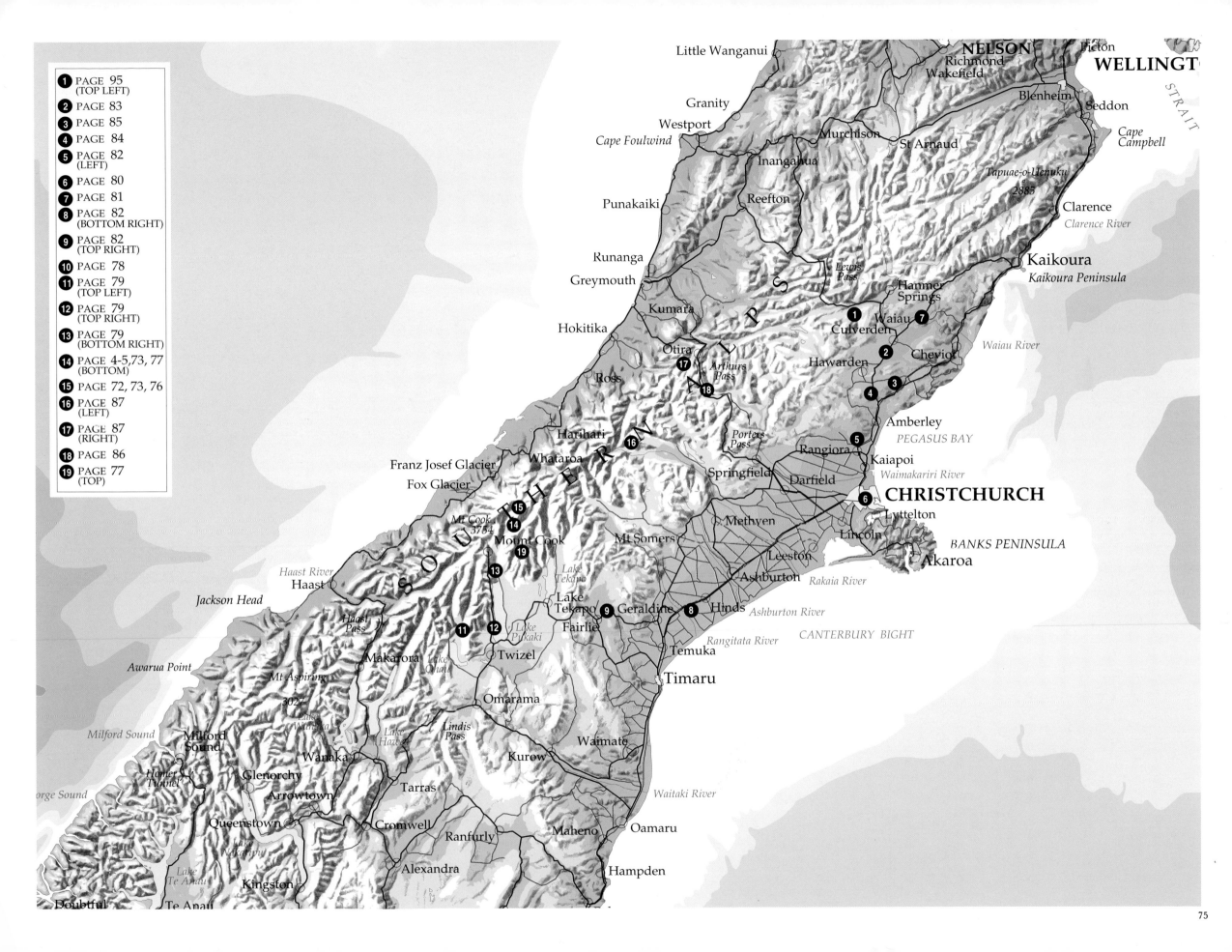

Little Wanganui

NELSON Picton
Richmond **WELLINGT**
Wakefield

Granity
Blenheim Seddon
Westport Murchison St Arnaud *Cape Campbell*
Cape Foulwind

Inangahua
Tapuae-o-Uenuku 2885

Punakaiki Reefton

Clarence
Clarence River

Runanga
Lewis Pass
Greymouth **Kaikoura**
Hanmer *Kaikoura Peninsula*
Springs
Kumara ① Waiau ⑦
Culverden *Waiau River*
Hokitika ②
Otira ⑰ Hawarden Cheviot
Ross ⑱ *Arthurs Pass* ④ ③
Amberley

Harihari *Porters Pass* ⑤ *PEGASUS BAY*
⑯ Rangiora
Whataroa Kaiapoi
Franz Josef Glacier *Waimakariri River*
Fox Glacier Springfield Darfield
CHRISTCHURCH
⑥
Lyttelton
⑮ Methven Lincoln
Mt Cook ⑭ *BANKS PENINSULA*
3754 Mount Cook Mt Somers Leeston **Akaroa**
⑲ Ashburton
Haast River Leeston
Haast ⑬ *Rakaia River*
Lake Tekapo
Jackson Head Lake
Tekapo ⑨ Geraldine ⑧ Hinds *Ashburton River*
Haast Pass Fairlie *CANTERBURY BIGHT*
Awarua Point ⑪ ⑫ *Lake Pukaki* Temuka *Rangitata River*
Makarora *Lake Ohau*
Mt Aspiring 3027 Twizel
Lake Hawea Lindis **Timaru**
Pass
Milford Sound Omarama Waimate
Milford Wanaka
Sound *Lake Wanaka* Kurow
Homer
Tunnel Glenorchy Tarras Maheno Oamaru
orge Sound Arrowtown
Queenstown Cromwell Ranfurly
Alexandra
Lake Te Anau Kingston Hampden
Doubtful Te Anau

75

The first tints of morning sun illuminate the eastern faces
of Mt Tasman.

The knife-edge crest of the Main Divide north of
Mt Tasman, with the head of the Tasman Glacier at the
top left.

Dense cloud blankets the Tasman and Murchison
Glaciers at about the level the ice surface would have
reached during the Ice Ages. Dominating the range
between the two glaciers is Mt Malte Brun (3156 m).

RIGHT: Climbers on the summit ice cap of Mt Cook.

An eccentric flourish in an otherwise reasonably predictable
eastern high country landscape — sharp pinnacles and ravines
eroded out of clay river cliffs in the Ahuriri River near Omarama.

During the Ice Ages the Mackenzie Basin was a vast dumping ground for moraine carried by huge glaciers that issued from the Godley, Tasman and Hopkins/Dobson Valleys. Since the ice began to retreat about 14,000 years ago, Lakes Tekapo, Pukaki and Ohau (ABOVE) have formed in the deep trenches carved by the vanished glaciers. Above the heads of these lakes, rivers like the Tasman (BOTTOM RIGHT) continue to transport debris eroded from the mountains down their broad, braided beds. During the 1970s and 1980s a major hydro-electricity scheme rearranged the topography of the area by raising the levels of the existing lakes, adding several artificial lakes and linking them all together with a network of large canals (TOP RIGHT).

FAR LEFT: Although increasingly encircled by tall modern office blocks, Christchurch's Cathedral Square still retains several splendid examples of the city's past devotion to gothic architecture, including the cathedral itself and the nearby offices of *The Press*.

TOP LEFT: Gothic buildings are also prominent in the region just west of Cathedral Square, including the Arts Centre (foreground) as well as the Canterbury Museum and Christ's College, both backing in to the leafy expanse of Hagley Park.

LOWER LEFT: Lawn bowls in progress in Hagley Park.

RIGHT: Sheep graze a Waiau Valley farm, North Canterbury.

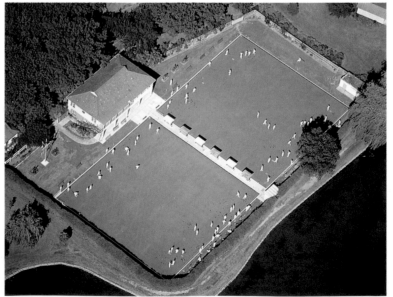

A patchwork of rectangular paddocks on the
Canterbury Plains gradually merges into the North
Canterbury foothills.

TOP: Sheep graze the rolling
South Canterbury hills between Geraldine
and Fairlie.

ABOVE: With a rainfall of only 500–750 mm
a year, irrigation is of critical importance for
agriculture on the dry Canterbury Plains.

Precision levelling and ridging of paddocks on the dry
Amuri Plain, near Culverden, part of a major gravity-fed
irrigation scheme utilising the waters of the nearby Waiau River.

Limestone outcrops and rolling hill paddocks near Weka Pass, between Waipara
and Waikari in North Canterbury.

North Canterbury farmland near the edge of the foothills. Closer examination of
the right hand side of the photograph reveals at least three levels of older
river terraces.

OPPOSITE: The headwaters of the Waimakariri River in Arthur's Pass National Park. After heavy rain the river spreads out over much of its bed, but in extended periods of dry weather it carries barely sufficient water for continuous surface flow.

ABOVE: The headwaters of the Rakaia River looking east. Prominent in the foreground is the Ramsay Glacier with its ice-tongue melting to form an expanding glacial lake.

RIGHT: The Kilmarnock Falls plunge down the steep side of Mt Davie in the southwestern corner of Arthur's Pass National Park.

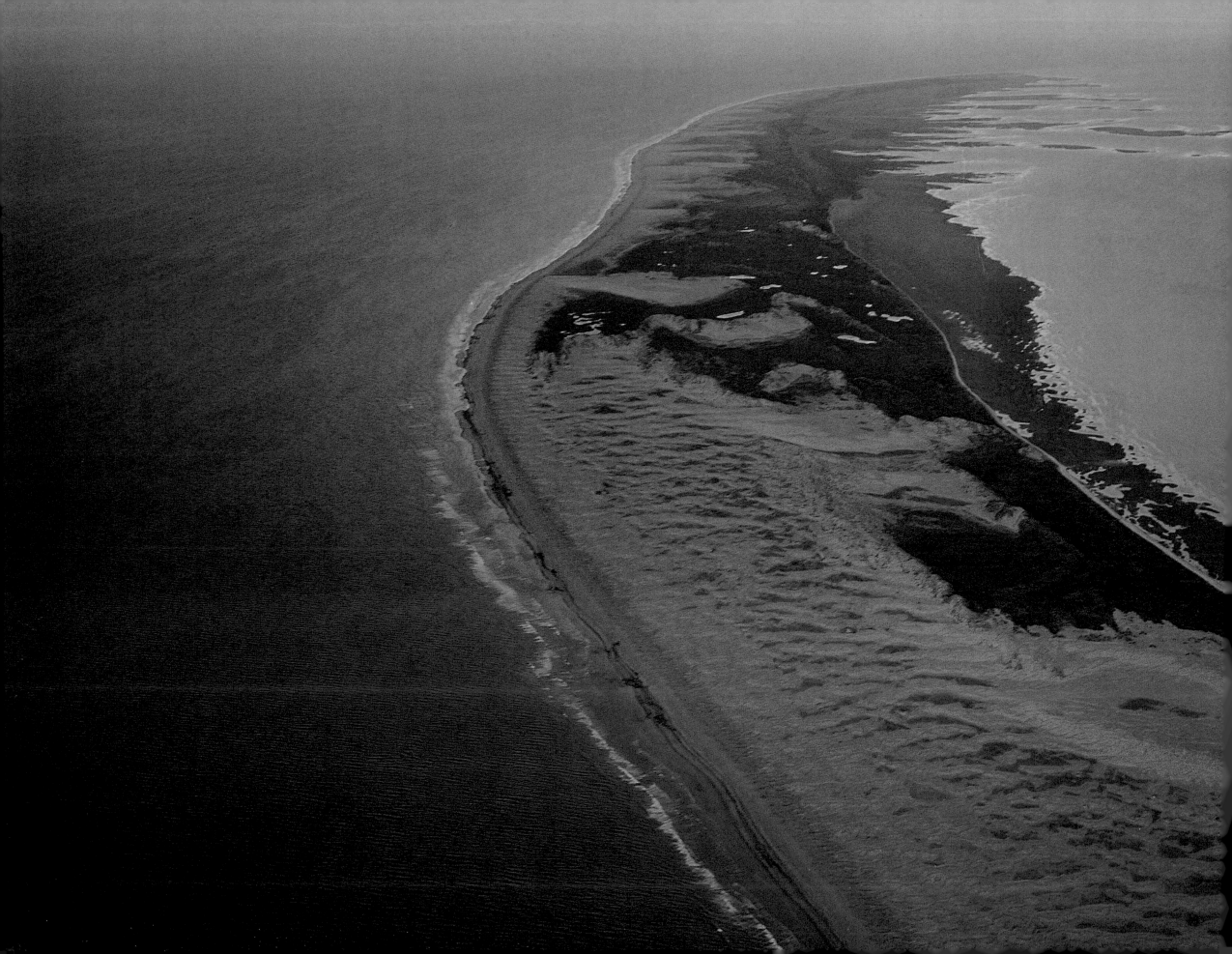

CHAPTER 4
Marlborough & Nelson

A fishing boat leaves
Nelson Haven at sunset.

OPPOSITE: Farewell
Spit, the remarkable
25 km sandspit at the
northwestern extremity
of the South Island.

IN TERMS of landforms, scenery and native
vegetation the Nelson–Marlborough region is
easily the most diverse part of New Zealand.
Although it has not produced a major tourist icon of
the status of Mt Cook or Milford Sound (with the
possible exception of the coastline of Abel Tasman
National Park), the region's salubrious climate, relaxed
lifestyle and wonderful spectrum of alpine and coastal
landscapes have made it one of the most desirable parts
of the country to live in and to visit.

The mountain systems of Nelson and
Marlborough are at the northern end of the Southern
Alps and remain tectonically very active. Scars from

major earthquakes are visible in the ranges of northwest Nelson, while to the east the Seaward and Inland Kaikouras are being pushed up more rapidly than any other segment of the New Zealand landmass. Paradoxically, these same crustal upheavals have slowly squeezed the steep-ridged hills of the Marlborough Sounds down into the sea, leaving a weaving system of drowned river valleys.

Geological variation and a wide range of climatic zones at the northern end of the South Island have resulted in the region's remarkable diversity of native plants and animals. Many southern plants, especially alpine species, reach their northern limits in the mountains of Nelson and Marlborough. Conversely, many northern species (including trees such as pukatea, titoki, whau and rewarewa) spill across Cook Strait to reach their southern limit in the warmer parts of the Nelson coastline and the Marlborough Sounds. The region is also the last refuge for native animals as weird and wonderful as the tuatara (the closest living relative of the dinosaurs), giant carnivorous land snails, and native frogs that lay no eggs, do not croak and have no webs between their toes.

The landscapes of Nelson–Marlborough do not easily fall into a simple descriptive sequence. In the southeast the Seaward Kaikoura mountains plunge from peaks of over 2600 m into deep ocean trenches within a few kilometres. Here major ocean currents meet in turbulent, sediment-laden seas, providing a rich habitat for a myriad of sea life, including massive groupings of playful dolphins and a small (though increasing) population of sperm whales.

Shelter from this exposed coast is found to the north in the Marlborough Sounds, a "labyrinth of waterways" that makes a superb recreational arena for boaties and holiday-makers. West of the Sounds the enclosing arms of Farewell Spit and, inland, a barrier of mountain ranges lend shelter to the relatively peaceful waters of Tasman and Golden Bays. Here the meeting of land and sea is more gentle, with many shallow sandy beaches, low barrier spits and large tidal estuaries. In the west of Tasman Bay the celebrated granite coastline of Abel Tasman National Park presents a sequence of rocky headlands interspersed with enchanting small, bush-fringed coves of golden sand, widely considered the loveliest small beaches anywhere in New Zealand.

Four huge, publicly owned blocks of mountain land make up much of this area's rugged interior: the arid, barren hills and mountains of the Inland Kaikoura Range and Molesworth Station; the bush-clad ridges of Mt Richmond Conservation Park; the mountains and beech-forested valleys of Nelson Lakes National Park; and the North West Nelson Conservation Park, easily the most diverse natural area anywhere in New Zealand.

In early times these inland places saw only occasional forays by human travellers — Maori on trails to the greenstone rivers of the West Coast, followed later by Europeans in search of gold or new pastures for their sheep. Settlement was, and still is, largely confined to the major flood-plain river valleys, such as the Wairau, Waimea, Motueka and Takaka valleys, and around coastal estuaries, where flat land and food was abundant.

Like most of New Zealand, Nelson–Marlborough has a primary economic base of sheep and dairy farming, as well as a long tradition of fruit growing. Lately this base has been broadened, with the harvesting of extensive exotic forests, the development of Port Nelson as the largest fish-processing port in New Zealand, the establishment of Marlborough at the centre of New Zealand's burgeoning wine industry and the growth in tourism. A constant expansion in the horticultural sector has revealed an array of products, from tropical orchids (sold back to tropical countries!) to new fruit crossbreeds.

Although the agreeable climate means that Nelson and Marlborough have their share of inhabitants who want little more than a place in the sun, the area has also attracted a colourful mixture of independent and creative people. Immigrants seeking a more benign lifestyle, a nationally renowned community of artists and crafts people, and followers of all manner of alternative lifestyles rub shoulders with the descendants of the original Maori and British colonists, giving the area a cultural diversity to match that found in its natural landscapes.

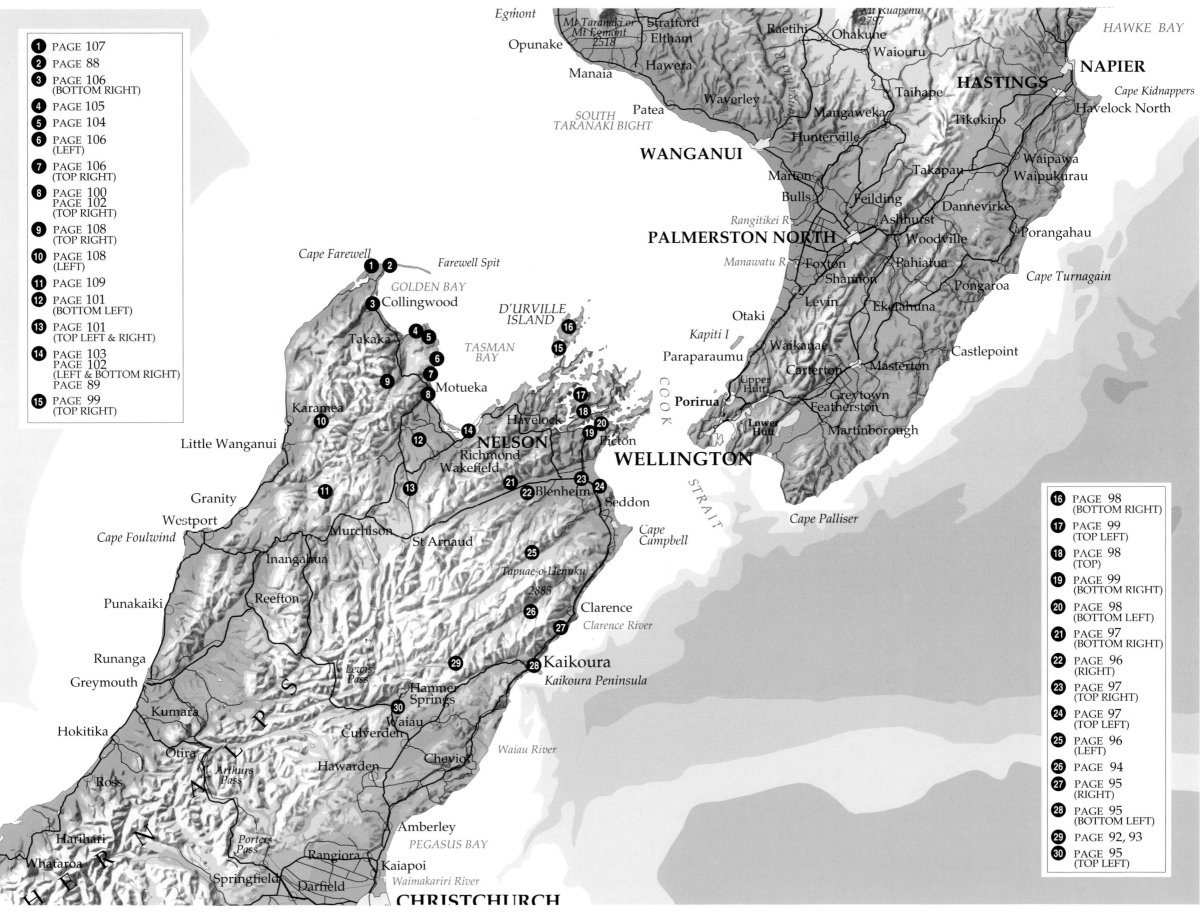

The Dillon River, a tributary of the Clarence River at the southern end of the
Inland Kaikoura Range, is part of the 1800 km² Molesworth Station, the largest
single pastoral land-holding anywhere in New Zealand.

OPPOSITE: The bare hills of Molesworth Station under a
coating of winter snow, looking northwards along the
Inland Kaikoura Range.

Arid hill country on the inland side of the Seaward Kaikoura Range.

ABOVE: Mt Alexander, with the Puhipuhi Valley to the left, in the eastern foothills of the Seaward Kaikoura Range.

TOP LEFT: A sidestream of the Waiau River just west of Hanmer Springs, with autumn colours scattered among the greens of pine plantations and invasions of introduced broom.

LEFT: The Kaikoura Peninsula, a limestone promontory with a flat top, and extensive reefs and marine life. The adjacent waters are one of the few places in the world where large whales can be seen in inshore waters throughout the year.

Dry hillsides of tussock grasses and broom in the Awatere Valley, inland Marlborough.

Farmland in the Wairau Valley, west of Blenheim.

ABOVE: One of the driest parts of the New Zealand coastline — the mouth of the Wairau River with the Opawa River winding down through the centre of the photograph.

TOP RIGHT: Dry pasture near the mouth of the Wairau River.

RIGHT: The braided bed of the Wairau River near Blenheim, with snow-capped Mt Fishtail prominent among the peaks of the Richmond Range in the background.

TOP: A view northwards over the complex labyrinth of ridges, waterways and islands of the outer parts of Pelorus Sound. ABOVE: The inter-island ferry in Queen Charlotte Sound.

The northern end of D'Urville Island, the largest of the islands in the Marlborough Sounds, with Port Hardy at the left.

ABOVE: Cleared hillsides reverting to scrub in the outer parts of Pelorus Sound. (This photograph portrays much of the same general area as the one at the top of page 98 — but from the opposite direction.)

TOP RIGHT: Clays and minerals sluiced from the hills add weird colouration to the waters of Greville Harbour on D'Urville Island in the aftermath of a cataclysmic storm.

BOTTOM RIGHT: The bays at the head of Port Underwood, with Tory Channel, Arapawa Island and the outer reaches of Queen Charlotte Sound beyond. Aerial photographs like this make it much easier to visualise the Marlborough Sounds as a network of valleys that are gradually being "drowned" as the land sinks slowly under the sea.

Deep friable soils along the lower reaches of the Motueka River that once grew
hops and tobacco now carry mainly kiwifruit and pip fruit orchards.

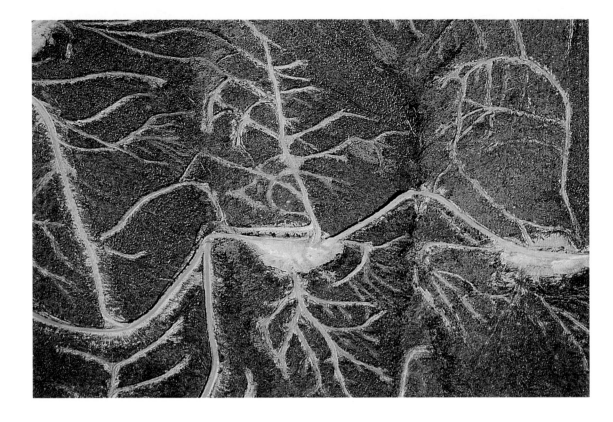

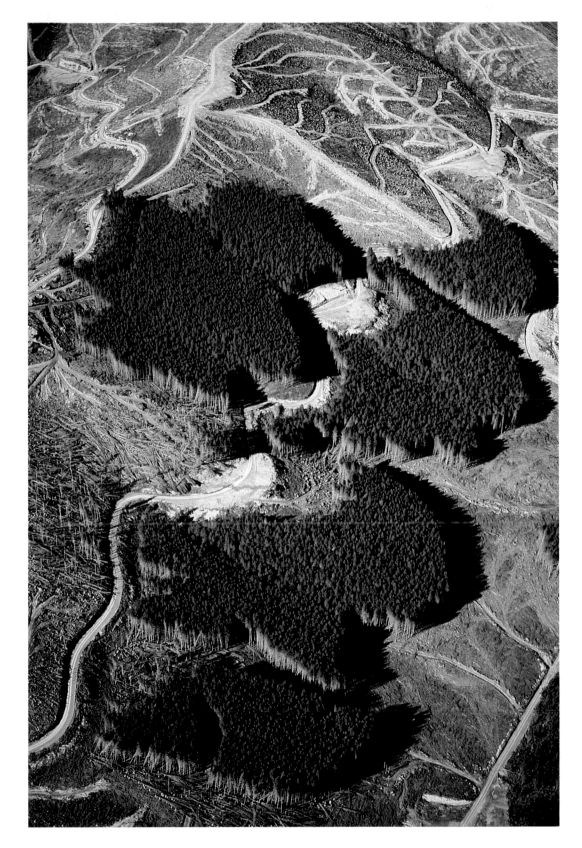

Low fertility soils on Nelson's Moutere Hills and Golden Downs have proved almost useless for farming but excellent for growing pines, eucalypts and other introduced trees. When the even-aged plantations mature, whole hillsides are usually felled and cleared for replanting.

Barrier sandspits are a common feature of the Nelson coast, but the 8 km Boulder Bank that encloses the tidal expanse of Nelson Haven is unique.

TOP: The geometrical precision of Motueka's horticultural grid becomes especially obvious in winter when, tidied and manicured, it awaits the release of spring.

ABOVE: The heart of Nelson City in late afternoon sunshine, with wooded Cathedral Hill in the centre of the photograph.

Nelson Haven, the Boulder Bank and Tasman Bay, with the hills of Abel
Tasman National Park in the distance.

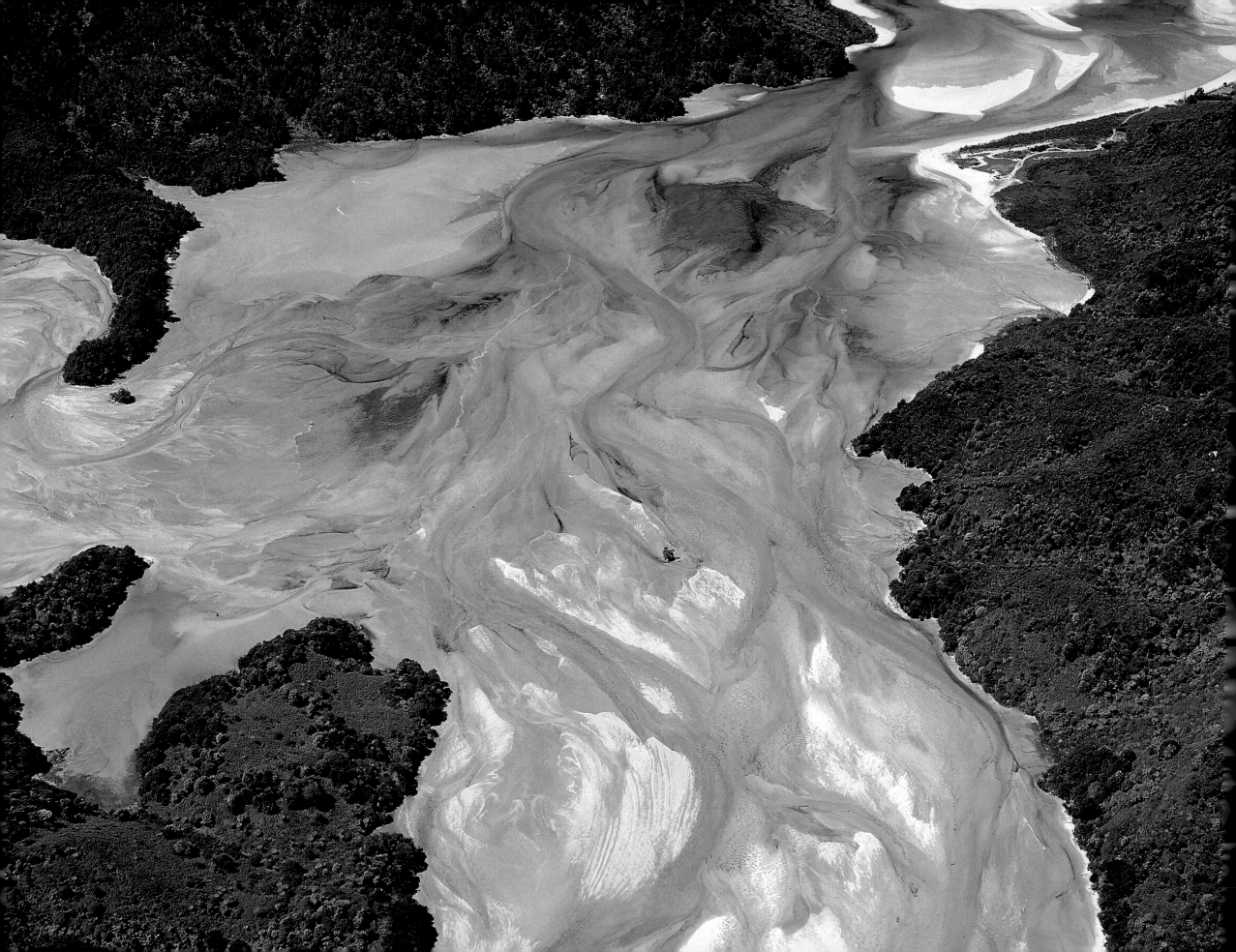

Sandbanks and clear stream channels in Awaroa (OPPOSITE) and Wainui Inlets,
at the Golden Bay end of Abel Tasman National Park.

The perfect crescent beaches of Te Pukatea and Anchorage Bays, Abel Tasman National Park.

TOP: Low tide at Marahau Beach.
ABOVE: Farmland north of Collingwood.

OPPOSITE: Archway Islands, off Wharariki Beach on the exposed west coast of Golden Bay.

Ice patterns in a frozen alpine lake near the Cobb Valley, North West Nelson Conservation Park.

LEFT: Vertical corrugations etched by acidic waters in limestone cliffs along the crest of the Garibaldi Ridge, a dramatic but little-visited region on the southern boundary of the Tasman Wilderness Area of North West Nelson Conservation Park.

OPPOSITE: The Hundred Acre (or Misery) Plateau on the Matiri Range, north of Murchison. This striking limestone tableland and encircling bluffs are just one example of a wide range of unusual karst (or limestone) landscapes that occur in the northwest Nelson region.

CHAPTER 5

Wellington, Wairarapa & Manawatu

Old and new buildings in the city centre display a contrast of architectural styles. The red-roofed Government Buildings, finished in 1876, is reputed to be the largest wooden building in the world. Behind is the modern dome-shaped "Beehive", which houses today's Parliament and ministerial offices.

OPPOSITE: New Zealand's capital city Wellington sprawls over steep hills and narrow valleys on the edge of the harbour.

THE SOUTHERN part of the North Island, and the Wellington region in particular, sits on top of several major, active fault lines; the inhabitants of New Zealand's capital city live "on the edge" both physically and psychologically. The city is rocked by frequent earthquakes, and Wellingtonians have somehow to cope with the inescapable fact that one day a major readjustment along one of these fault lines is likely to shake the city to its foundations.

The last really big earthquake in these parts occurred in 1855 and raised the central areas of

Wellington City and the lower section of the Hutt Valley about 2 m, creating at the same time the sea-shelf that today carries the Hutt Motorway. In an area dominated by steep hills and narrow valleys, this "new" flat land came as a godsend to early European settlers, who quickly put it to use as the site for Wellington's main business centre and port. What the early settlers didn't realise, though, as they built, out of brick and granite, a city with splendid Victorian architecture, was that the earthquakes would continue. More recently, a local body ultimatum has forced the strengthening or destruction of some 700 of the most-at-risk brick structures in the downtown area. Now Wellington's modern city centre of glass and steel stands high and defiant, although no-one really knows how either the buildings or the reclaimed land on which they stand will respond to major earth tremors in the future.

New Zealand's capital was shifted to Wellington from Auckland in 1865, with the aim of creating a more centrally based government for the country. Today Greater Wellington (including Porirua and the Hutt Valley) is our second-largest urban area, with a population about a third the size of Auckland's. It is the seat of Parliament and centre for government departments and many companies. A cosmopolitan city, it has a high concentration of many of the country's ethnic minorities — European, Pacific and Asian. Its reputation as one of the world's windiest cities is not without reason: gales blast Wellington on average 40 days a year, regularly putting the airport and inter-island ferry service out of action.

Stretching north from Wellington, the Rimutaka, Tararua and Ruahine Ranges form an almost continuous mountainous backbone for this southern region, broken only by the deep cleft of the Manawatu Gorge. Rugged and thickly clothed with mixed beech forest, the ranges are popular places for trampers, hunters and day-trippers. Either side of the ranges, the land is almost completely denuded of its original forest cover, having been cleared for timber, farming and settlement.

Unlike most of New Zealand, where the west coast is characteristically wild and rugged and the east coast softer and tamer, in this region the pattern is confused. A token expression of the kind of coastline normally associated with the western parts of New Zealand is found in the southwestern corner of the region, where, west of Wellington, cliffs rise steeply and dramatically from the rocky shoreline. This more abrupt coastline soon terminates, and the west coast extends northwards in long sandy stretches, backed by coastal flats of rich alluvial soils cultivated for market gardening and mixed cropping, behind which hills are grazed by sheep and cattle. The Manawatu, with its main city of Palmerston North, is one of the most fertile and intensively farmed regions of New Zealand, providing food for both local and export markets.

East of the Tararua and Rimutaka Ranges the broad plain of the Wairarapa, with its well-groomed farms, elegant rural mansions and pleasant towns, presents one of the more prosperous faces of pastoral New Zealand. This valley is the southernmost of a series of fertile farming basins running more or less directly up the centre of this part of the North Island into Hawke's Bay, aligned on the fault that defines the eastern edge of the central mountain chain. The settlements that service this area — such as Martinborough, Featherston, Eketahuna and Pahiatua — epitomise the durable conservative character of many rural New Zealand townships.

To the east, between these basins and the sea, the landscape becomes much less hospitable, with steep, bare, dissected hill country ending, often abruptly, at probably the wildest and most desolate stretch of coastline in the entire North Island. Running for over 350 km from Cape Kidnappers in the north down to Cape Palliser on the exposed southeastern corner of the North Island, this coast has no sheltered harbours and only a handful of small settlements, and its drama and isolation offer a compelling counter-balance to the more populous country to the west.

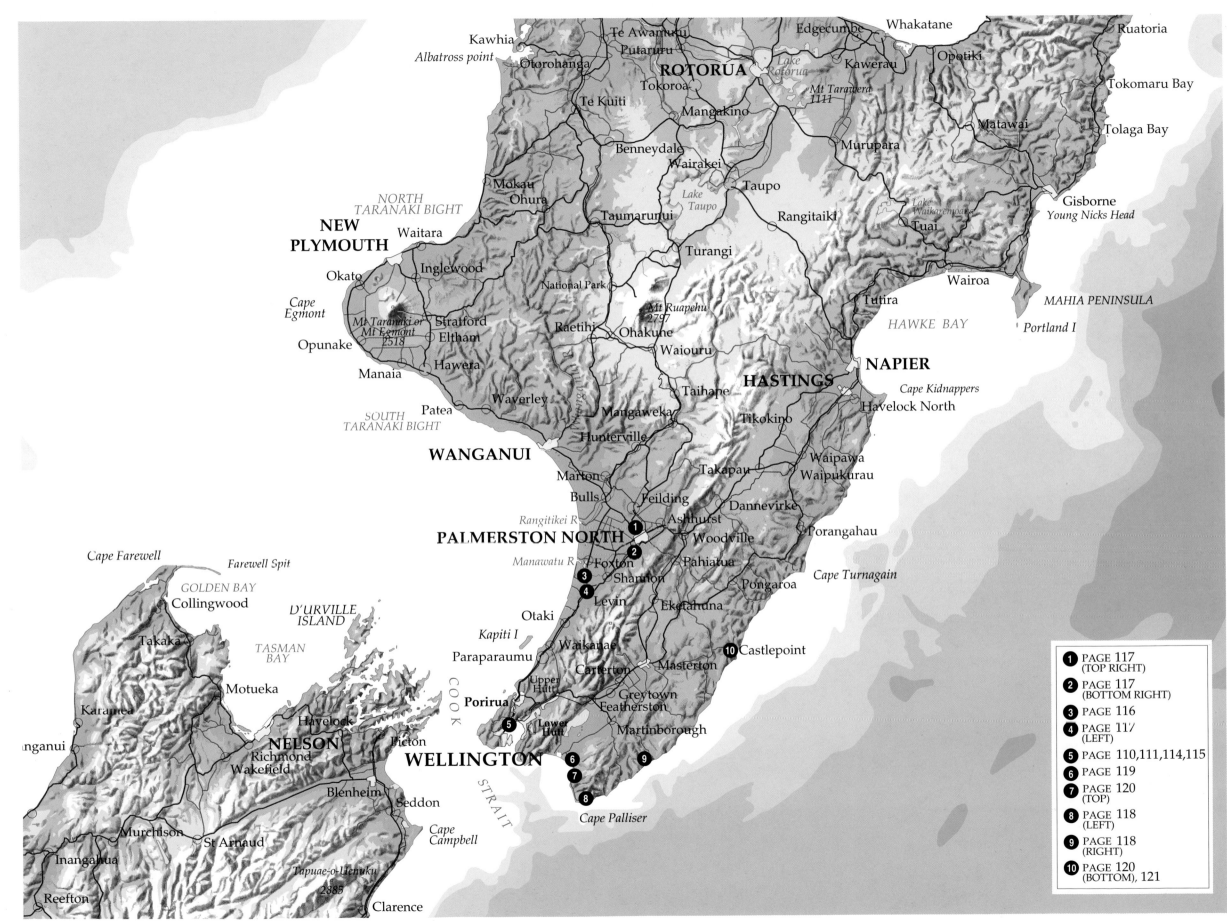

Kawhia
Albatross point
Te Awamutu
Putaruru
ROTORUA
Lake Rotorua
Edgecumbe
Whakatane
Ruatoria
Opotiki
Tokomaru Bay
Otorohanga
Tokoroa
Mt Tarawera 1111
Kawerau
Te Kuiti
Mangakino
Murupara
Matawai
Tolaga Bay
Benneydale
Wairakei
NORTH TARANAKI BIGHT
Mokau
Ohura
Taupo
Lake Taupo
Rangitaiki
Tuai
Lake Waikaremoana
Gisborne
Young Nicks Head
Taumarunui
NEW PLYMOUTH
Waitara
Turangi
Okato
Inglewood
National Park
Mt Ruapehu 2797
Wairoa
MAHIA PENINSULA
Portland I
Cape Egmont
Mt Taranaki or Mt Egmont 2518
Stratford
Eltham
Raetihi
Ohakune
NAPIER
HAWKE BAY
Opunake
Waiouru
HASTINGS
Cape Kidnappers
Manaia
Hawera
Taihape
Havelock North
Waverley
Mangaweka
Tikokino
SOUTH TARANAKI BIGHT
Patea
Hunterville
Waipawa
Waipukurau
WANGANUI
Marton
Takapau
Bulls
Feilding
Dannevirke
Rangitikei R
Ashhurst
Porangahau
PALMERSTON NORTH
Woodville
Manawatu R
Foxton
Pahiatua
Cape Farewell
Farewell Spit
Shannon
Pongaroa
Cape Turnagain
GOLDEN BAY
Levin
Ekatahuna
Collingwood
Otaki
D'URVILLE ISLAND
TASMAN BAY
Kapiti I
Waikanae
Castlepoint
Takaka
Paraparaumu
Masterton
Carterton
Motueka
COOK
Upper Hutt
Greytown
Featherston
Karamea
Porirua
Lower Hutt
Martinborough
anganui
NELSON
Richmond
Wakefield
Havelock
Picton
WELLINGTON
STRAIT
Cape Palliser
Blenheim
Seddon
Cape Campbell
Murchison
St Arnaud
Inangahua
Tapuae-o-Uenuku 2885
Reefton
Clarence

1 PAGE 117 (TOP RIGHT)
2 PAGE 117 (BOTTOM RIGHT)
3 PAGE 116
4 PAGE 117 (LEFT)
5 PAGE 110,111,114,115
6 PAGE 119
7 PAGE 120 (TOP)
8 PAGE 118 (LEFT)
9 PAGE 118 (RIGHT)
10 PAGE 120 (BOTTOM), 121

Oriental Parade is Wellington's brief stretch of Riviera, and its
clustered wooden houses and concrete towers house some of the
city's rich and famous.

ABOVE: Painted tin roofs of a Wellington suburb — a scene that
could be found in any New Zealand town or city.

RIGHT TOP: Southeast Wellington, with the National Museum
and Basin Reserve in the foreground and the Miramar Peninsula
in the distance.

RIGHT BOTTOM: The heart of Wellington City, looking south
through Newtown towards Island Bay.

Ploughed fields near Levin, where rich alluvial soils support intensive
market gardening.

ABOVE & RIGHT BOTTOM: The fertile coastal plains of the Horowhenua and Manawatu regions were once covered in magnificent native forests. Today the forests have been replaced by lush dairy pasture and market gardens that supply much of Wellington's milk and vegetables.

TOP: Shelterbelts protect young kiwifruit vines growing on the rich silty soils of the Manawatu.

Burnt trees near Cape Palliser, a stark reminder of the days when European pioneers put a match to vast areas of hill country forest in the Wairarapa region.

A rock reef near Castle Point.

OPPOSITE: Once-forested hills near Cape Palliser now stand bare and dry in the midsummer heat. A former seabed uplifted by the movement of the earth's underlying plates, the land has eroded quickly into steep valleys and trenches.

Part of the southern Wairarapa coast near Cape Palliser, a place of spectacular beaches, good fishing and a sunny, dry climate. Cape Palliser is the southernmost point in the North Island, on about the same latitude as Blenheim and Westport in the South Island.

OPPOSITE: The lighthouse at Castle Point, named by Captain Cook in 1770 because the cliffs that rise abruptly from the sea looked like castle ramparts. Castle Point was an important port for the Wairarapa until the District was linked to the Main Trunk railway in the 1880s.

Fishers try their luck from the cliff edge at Castle Point, one of the favourite coastal haunts for the people of Masterton and other inland Wairarapa towns.

CHAPTER 6
Hawke's Bay, East Cape & Urewera

Before Captain Cook renamed it, local Maori tribes called Cape Kidnappers Te-Matau-a-Maui, the fish-hook of Maui. Its sharp edges, adzed by weather and sea, reminded them of the legendary fish-hook with which Maui "fished up" the North Island. Australasian gannets have made Cape Kidnappers one of their main nesting areas in New Zealand.

THE RUGGED and inaccessible Raukumara Range and the dense forested wilderness of the Urewera combine to create a formidable barrier that cuts much of this eastern region off from the rest of the North Island; for many years the only access to the East Cape was by sea. Today, even though a tortuous road winds around the coastline from the Bay of Plenty to Gisborne, and roads cut through the centre of the Urewera, the East Cape remains remote and sparsely populated. The Raukumara Range rises, with line upon line of imposing ridges, as the backdrop to the region, a wild and brooding hinterland that visitors are advised not to enter without local knowledge. The exposed seaward flanks of the range, stripped bare of forest, fall steeply to a spectacular coastline that forms the easternmost extremity of New Zealand. Mt Hikurangi (1752 m), the highest point on the range and the highest non-volcanic peak in the North Island, is said to be the first place on earth each day to be warmed by the rays of the morning sun.

Although Captain James Cook made his first New Zealand landfall in 1769 near Gisborne, the region's inaccessibility and rugged nature made it one of the last parts of the country to be settled by Europeans. Consequently the East Cape and Urewera Country have remained as strongholds of Maori life and culture. The land is imbued with Maori legend and spirituality, and most small rural communities are centred on the traditional marae and meeting house. Today, Maori make up more than half of the East Cape's rural population, and more than a third of the population of Gisborne, the East Cape's main urban centre. In the Urewera district, the Tuhoe, the Children of the Mist, have kept more separate from European culture, lifestyle and religion than any other Maori tribe. In the early part of this century, a settlement of over 2000 people flourished in the heart of this remote maze of densely forested ridges, drawn

together by the Tuhoe prophet Rua Kenana. Rua's followers, the Wairua Tau, were the last Maori to try to achieve complete political, social and economic independence from Pakeha New Zealand.

South of the Raukumara Range, the Urewera wilderness is the largest remaining expanse of native forest in the North Island. Much of it is high-altitude beech forest, protected in the 211,000 ha Urewera National Park. Nearby, although not included in the park, are the magnificent rainforests of Whirinaki, the tallest and densest stands of podocarp trees left in New Zealand. Whirinaki's forests inspired conservationists to fight a major campaign in the 1970s to protect them from logging. These remnants are a living museum of the great Gondwanaland rainforests that once covered much of the fertile lowlands of the North Island.

Tucked at the foot of the East Cape on the eastern edge of the Urewera wilderness, and in sharp contrast, are the lush plains of Hawke's Bay. Once covered in native forest, the fertile land now yields vegetables, grains and fruits, and the treeless plains are an orderly patchwork of fields and crops. Unlike the forested interior, where a high annual rainfall (some 2000 mm a year) rivals parts of the South Island's notorious West Coast, the Hawke's Bay coastal flats bask in some of the country's sunniest and driest weather. The region's two main cities, Napier and Hastings, and the

surrounding rural areas enjoy a wealth founded on the fat of the land, and reflect their British heritage in architecture and lifestyle, and in the hunting and horse breeding of wealthy landowners.

Most of the first Europeans to settle this area were sheep farmers, many of them moving north from the Wairarapa. Their arrival in this region resulted in the usual legacy of cleared forest and scarred hills, but here the consequences have been more severe than in most other parts of New Zealand. Every time an intense rainstorm hits the coast, extensive slipping occurs in the hills and huge volumes of soil get washed away. In 1988, Cyclone Bola swept away vast quantities from the hills throughout the region, burying orchards and farmland on the coastal lowlands and leaving as a legacy of the storm a two-metre deep mud slick moving across the sea floor and sliding off the continental shelf.

Despite this, the steep, bare flanks of the East Cape's coastal hills have a dramatic beauty all their own, especially when low early-morning light touches the bare contours of this young landscape. Anyone who takes on the winding 340 km journey around the coastline between Opotiki and Gisborne, with its spectacular rocky headlands and deserted beaches, is constantly reminded that those places that are hardest to get to often bring the greatest rewards.

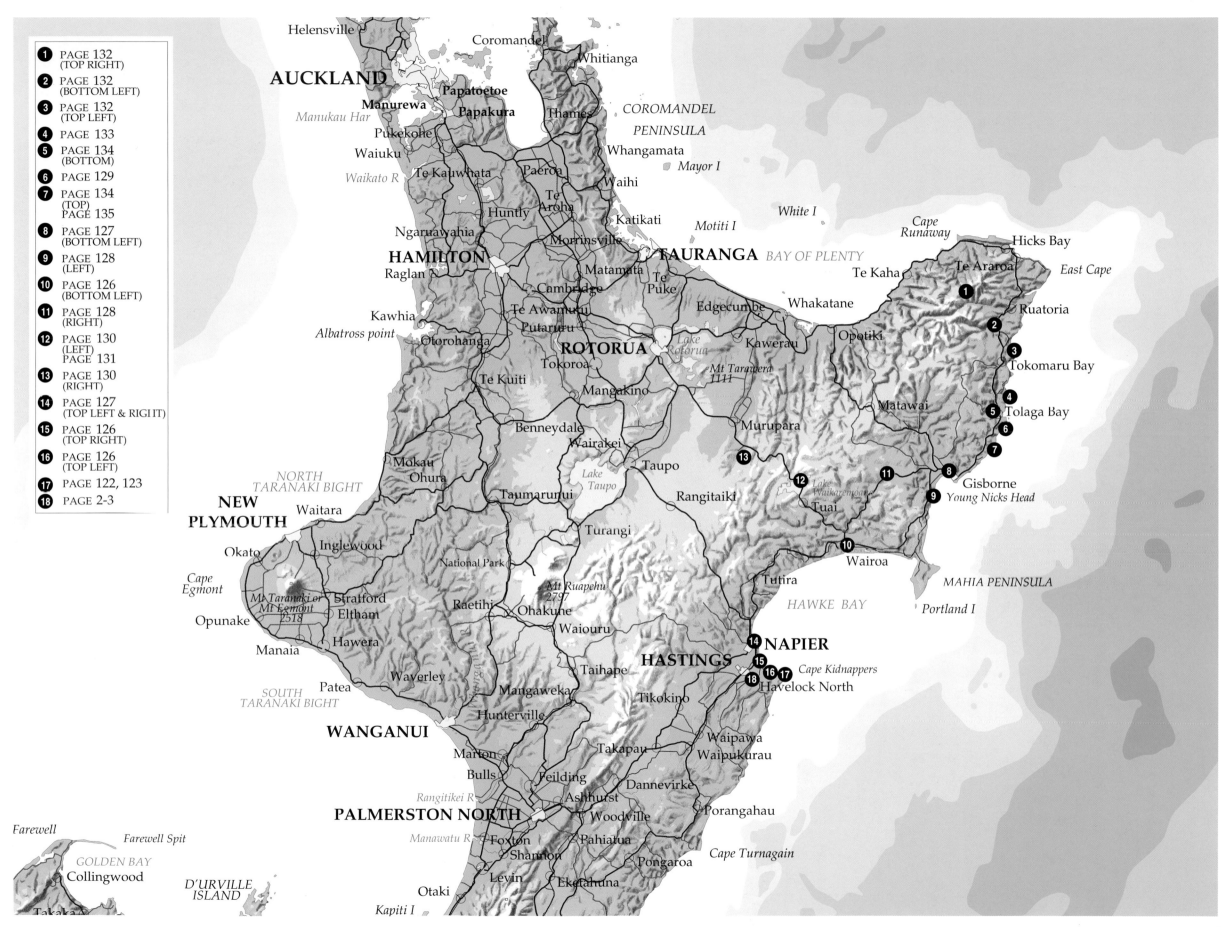

Helensville

Coromandel

Whitianga

AUCKLAND

Manurewa **Papatoetoe**

Manukau Har **Papakura** Thames *COROMANDEL*

Pukekohe

Waiuku Whangamata *PENINSULA*

Waikato R Waihi *Mayor I*

Te Kauwhata Paeroa

Te Waihi

Huntly Aroha Katikati White I *Cape*

Runaway

Ngaruawahia Morrinsville *Motiti I* Hicks Bay

HAMILTON *BAY OF PLENTY* Te Araroa

Raglan Matamata **TAURANGA** Te Kaha *East Cape*

Te Cambridge Te Ruatoria

Kawhia Puke Edgecumbe Opotiki

Te Awamutu Whakatane Kawerau Tokomaru Bay

Albatross point Putaruru

Otorohanga **ROTORUA** *Lake* Matawai Tolaga Bay

Rotorua Kawerau

Te Kuiti Tokoroa *Mt Tarawera* Murupara

1111 Gisborne

Benneydale Mangakino Tuai *Young Nicks Head*

Wairakei

Mokau *Lake* Taupo Rangitaiki

NORTH Ohura *Taupo*

TARANAKI BIGHT Taumarunui Wairoa

Waitara Turangi *MAHIA PENINSULA*

NEW

PLYMOUTH National Park Tutira *Portland I*

Okato Inglewood *HAWKE BAY*

Cape *Mt Ruapehu*

Egmont *Mt Taranaki or* Stratford *2797*

Mt Egmont Eltham Raetihi

Opunake *2518* Ohakune

Manaia Waiouru **NAPIER**

Hawera **HASTINGS** *Cape Kidnappers*

Waverley Taihape Havelock North

SOUTH Patea

TARANAKI BIGHT Mangaweka Waipawa

WANGANUI Hunterville Tikokino Waipukurau

Marton Takapau

Bulls Dannevirke Porangahau

Feilding

PALMERSTON NORTH Woodville *Cape Turnagain*

Rangitikei R Ashhurst Pahiatua

Manawatu R Foxton *Manawatu R*

Farewell *Farewell Spit* Shannon Pongaroa

Levin Eketahuna

GOLDEN BAY Otaki

Collingwood *D'URVILLE*

ISLAND *Kapiti I*

Takaka

ABOVE: Aerial perspectives yield sudden visual surprises — a field of grains drying in the sun becomes an intriguing abstract design.

TOP LEFT: Bare hills near Cape Kidnappers.

LEFT: As it nears the sea at the northern Hawke's Bay town of Wairoa, the Wairoa River cuts wide, meandering curves across its valley floor. After heavy rains its waters turn murky brown from the large quantities of topsoil that get washed off the deforested and slip-prone hill country that makes up most of its extensive catchment.

ABOVE: Like many of New Zealand's provincial towns, Gisborne is sited where a sizeable spread of level country coincides with the mouth of a navigable river.

TOP & RIGHT: A prosperous community with a relaxed, seaside lifestyle and high sunshine hours, Napier is the sixth largest provincial city in New Zealand and a popular holiday centre.

Rich, fertile plains south of Gisborne stretch out towards
Young Nicks Head.

Sheep pasture on corrugated hill country near the
Hangaroa River, inland from Gisborne.

Shifting sheep to new pasture near Tolaga Bay.

Kahikatea trees up to 60 m tall near Minginui in Whirinaki Forest Park encircle the Arahaki Lagoon, a natural frost flat that fills with water in heavy rain. Forest like this was once found in many parts of New Zealand, but it is now difficult to find a reasonable stand of kahikatea outside South Westland, let alone one as impressive as this.

LEFT & OPPOSITE: Virgin beech forests surround Lake Waikareiti in Urewera National Park, with sacred Lake Waikaremoana in the background. Except for these lakes, virtually the whole of the park is covered by forest, the largest area of native forest left in the North Island.

ABOVE: Sunrise from the Raukumara Range, whose highest peak, Mt Hikurangi, is claimed to be the first place on earth to see the sun of each new day. The range creates an almost impenetrable barrier between the Bay of Plenty and Gisborne regions.

TOP LEFT: The Maori meeting house and marae at Waipiro Bay, a small farming community on the East Cape. In the early 1900s Waipiro Bay was the region's largest settlement and a major port of call for ships plying the coast.

LEFT: A school bus travels the coast road near Ruatoria, servicing the small coastal communities of this sparsely populated region.

OPPOSITE: Marau Point looking south to Tolaga Bay. Steep, barren hills rising straight from the edge of the sea and lines of surf rolling in on deserted sandy beaches make this a spectacular coastline.

LEFT & OPPOSITE: Gable End Foreland, north of Gisborne, was named by Captain James Cook in October 1769 "on account of the very great resemblance the white cliff has to the gable end of a house". The smooth face of the cliff is the result of erosion stripping away softer mudstones from layers of more resistant rock in strata that were originally deposited horizontally but have since been stood on end.

Looking like some strange primeval insect, Tolaga Bay's concrete jetty is a legacy of an era when the bay was a busy East Coast port and settlement.

CHAPTER 7
Taranaki, Wanganui, Taupo & The Bay Of Plenty

Mt Ruapehu's crater lake surrounded by winter snow.

OPPOSITE: The calm blue-grey waters of Mt Ruapehu's crater lake mask the dangerous subterranean powers that lie beneath. Lake temperatures change rapidly from lukewarm to boiling hot, and water periodically bursts out from the crater, causing huge mudflows known as lahars.

IN MAORI legend, the central North Island was once the home of great mountainous gods. Tongariro, Ngauruhoe, Ruapehu and Taranaki were tall, proud males with impressive snowy flanks, standing together in the centre of the country and competing for the love of the only female in their midst. The beautiful Pihanga, a graceful mountain goddess with soft gentle slopes and a thick cloak of deep green forest around her, favoured the mighty Tongariro, but Taranaki, madly in love, still sought her attentions.

137

A huge conflict broke out between Tongariro and Taranaki, and the mountain gods erupted in anger, darkening the sky. In the battle, Tongariro lost much of his height, but emerged victorious at the side of his beloved Pihanga. Taranaki, grieving, fled west towards the setting sun, carving a deep furrow in the earth, until he eventually came to rest on the west coast. There he stands today in isolated splendour, while the wound he gouged in the earth flows with the healing waters of the Whanganui River.

The fiery mountain gods still dominate the landscape of the central North Island, a zone of active volcanism that stretches from Mt Taranaki in the west to White Island off the Bay of Plenty coast. There are regular eruptions on Mt Tongariro and Mt Ruapehu as well as on White Island, and more than once in the past hundred or so years the gods have given vent to their anger with tragic results. The eruption of Mt Tarawera, near Rotorua, in June 1886 and the collapse of a volcanic plug in Mt Ruapehu's crater lake on Christmas Eve 1953 each caused the loss of over 150 lives. But these were only minor events compared to the colossal explosive eruptions that have taken place in the distant past at Rotorua and Taupo. These have occurred, on average, once every 30,000 years, and the most recent, at Taupo in AD 186, is thought to be the most violent volcanic eruption anywhere in the world in historical times. It is estimated to have been 30 times the size of the Mt St Helens eruption in 1980 and 12 times bigger that Krakatoa in 1883, and its

influence on sunsets in the Northern Hemisphere was recorded in both Roman and Chinese annals.

Along with its regular eruptions and the huge scale of its past volcanic events, what makes this region especially interesting is the fact that most major types of volcano and volcanic landforms are found here. Moreover, a good deal of activity has taken place in comparatively recent times, so that weathering and erosion have had only limited impact and many of the landforms remain more or less as they emerged from the inferno. The classic andesitic cones of Mt Taranaki, Mt Ngauruhoe, Mt Edgecumbe and White Island, the domes and craters of Mt Tarawera, the Rotorua caldera, the symmetrical ring-plain encircling Mt Taranaki, the vast ignimbrite sheets of the Mamaku and Kaingaroa plateaux, and the widespread lava flows and deposits of pumice and ash all provide textbook examples of what happens when the earth's molten interior blasts out through the surface crust.

Over the millenia an estimated 12,000 km^3 of volcanic material has been deposited on the surrounding landscape, accumulating in layers up to 4000 m deep and extending as far north as Auckland. The lush dairy pastures that encircle Mt Taranaki and the extensive kiwifruit orchards scattered over much of the Bay of Plenty lowlands both provide ample testimony to the high fertility of some of the soils that have developed on this widespread volcanic fallout.

However, on the Volcanic Plateau itself, the soils

initially seemed to be unsuitable for agriculture, and, until the deficiencies were identified, vast areas north of Lake Taupo were planted in fast-growing introduced pines in what became the largest afforestation scheme anywhere in the world. In the 1950s towns such as Kawerau and Kinleith rapidly expanded to service these huge plantings and provide a work force for a major pulp and paper industry. These productive forests have also helped to boost Tauranga's status as New Zealand's major export port.

Besides the volcanoes, innumerable hot springs, seething pools of boiling mud, steaming fumaroles, explosive geysers and beautiful silica sculptures are dotted over much of the central North Island, surface manifestations of the natural hot-water systems that often occur in conjunction with zones of active volcanism. The city of Rotorua is a major thermal phenomenon, its 55,000 inhabitants residing on the lid of a steaming pressure cooker and resigned to the ever-present odour of hydrogen sulphide. Many businesses and homes in Rotorua are piped into the natural hot-water supply bubbling away beneath their floor-boards. New Zealand has pioneered electricity generation from geothermal sources, though the real boon these exotic natural phenomena have brought is tourism. Summer walking and winter skiing on the volcanoes, boating and fishing on Lakes Taupo and Rotorua, and sightseeing at the geysers and mudpools bring large numbers of visitors to this New Zealand "zone of fire".

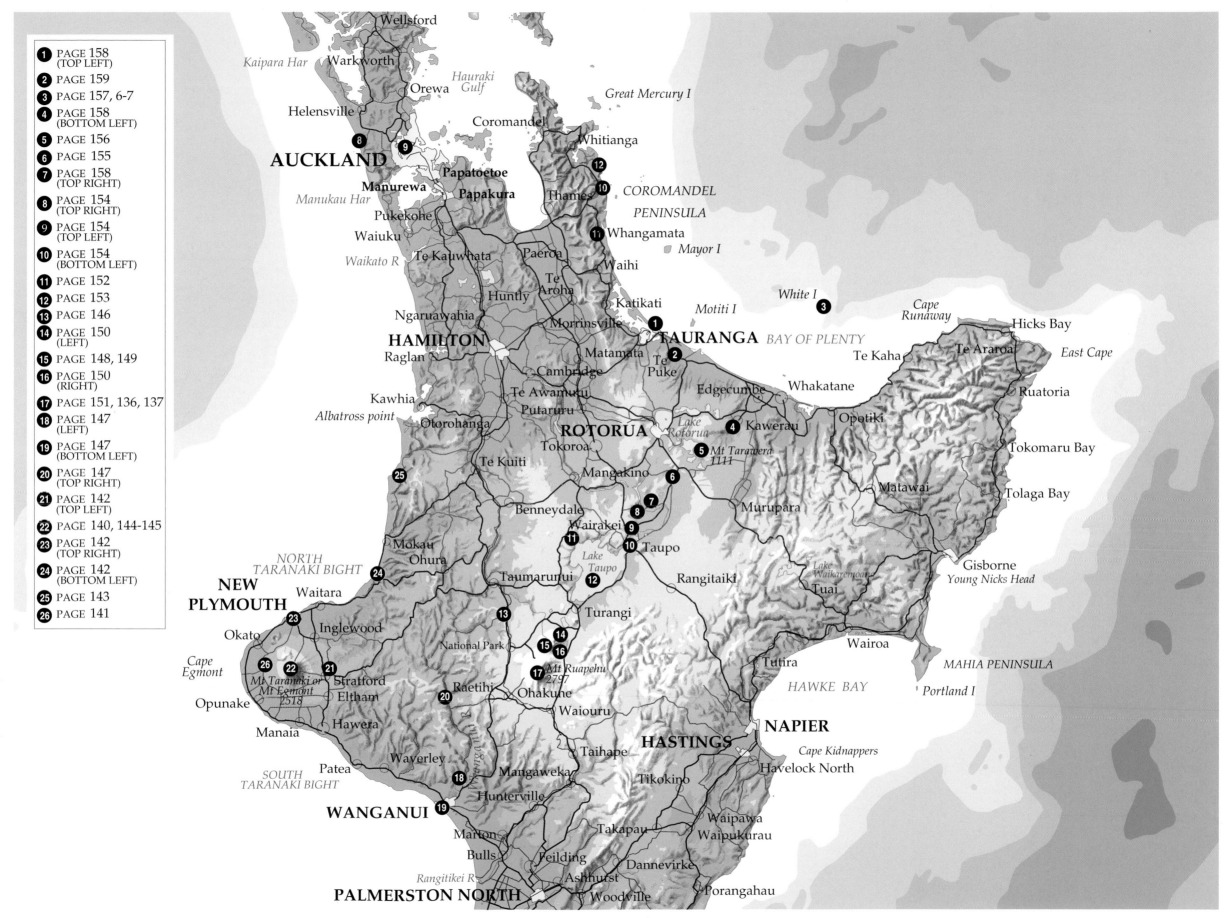

Wellsford

Kaipara Har Warkworth

Orewa

Helensville

Hauraki Gulf

Great Mercury I

Coromandel

Whitianga

8 AUCKLAND 9

Papatoetoe

12

10 *COROMANDEL*

Manurewa Papakura Thames *PENINSULA*

Manukau Har

Pukekohe

11 Whangamata

Waiuku

Mayor I

Waikato R Te Kauwhata Paeroa

Waihi

Te Aroha

Katikati

Motiti I

White I

Huntly Morrinsville

3

1 *Cape Runaway*

Hicks Bay

Ngaruawahia

TAURANGA *BAY OF PLENTY*

Te Kaha Te Araroa

East Cape

HAMILTON

2

Matamata Te Puke

Raglan

Te Araroa

Cambridge

Whakatane

Ruatoria

Te Awamutu Edgecumbe

Kawhia Putaruru

4 Kawerau Opotiki

Albatross point Otorohanga

ROTORUA *Lake Rotorua*

Tokomaru Bay

Tokoroa

5 Mt Tarawera 1111

Te Kuiti

Mangakino

25 6 Matawai Tolaga Bay

Benneydale

7 Murupara

Mokau 8

9

Wairakei

Lake Waikaremoana

11 10 Taupo

Gisborne *Young Nicks Head*

NORTH TARANAKI BIGHT

Ohura

Lake Taupo

12 Tuai

SOUTH TARANAKI BIGHT

24 Taumarunui

Rangitaiki

NEW PLYMOUTH Waitara

23 Inglewood

13 Turangi

Wairoa

MAHIA PENINSULA

Okato

National Park

14

15 16

HAWKE BAY

Tutira

Cape Egmont

26 22 21 Stratford

Raetihi

17 Mt Ruapehu 2797

Portland I

Mt Taranaki or Mt Egmont 2518 Eltham

20 Ohakune

Opunake

Waiouru

NAPIER

Manaia Hawera

Taihape

HASTINGS *Cape Kidnappers*

Waverley

Mangaweka Tikokino Havelock North

Patea 18

South Taranaki Bight Hunterville

Waipawa

19 Marton Waipukurau

WANGANUI Bulls Feilding Dannevirke

Rangitikei R Ashhurst Porangahau

PALMERSTON NORTH Woodville

Old Maori fortifications on the summits of lava domes near Parihaka.

The coastal plain near New Plymouth has been built up by showers of volcanic ash and eroded by many small streams that radiate from Mt Taranaki.

OPPOSITE: The last rays of the setting sun illuminate the summit cone of Mt Taranaki (2518 m), a dormant andesitic volcano that last erupted about 1775.

The tiny Maori settlement of Parihaka lives on as a symbol of passive resistance in New Zealand. During the land wars of the 1870s, local tribes used peaceful means to defend their land and people against European attack. The distinctive domes on the lava plain that surrounds Parihaka are bubbles that formed in the quickly cooling lava.

Built on an old lava flow from Mt Taranaki, New Plymouth has become a centre for energy exploration and production.

TOP LEFT: Farmland near Stratford. A generous amount of rain coupled with the fertile soils that have developed on the ring-plain that encircles Mt Taranaki have made this one of New Zealand's most productive dairy farming districts.

LEFT: Dramatic coastal bluffs north of New Plymouth where a grey band of older mudstones has been overlaid with a layer of volcanic ash erupted from Mt Taranaki.

OPPOSITE: Tirua Point on the north Taranaki coastline. While heavy swells cut into the coastal cliffs, clouds bank up on the hills in response to the prevailing westerly airstream.

OVERLEAF: Mt Taranaki from the west, catching the golden light of the setting sun, with the secondary crater of Fanthams Peak to the right.

Early morning mist wreathes valleys near Taumarunui in the headwaters of the
Whanganui River. The land has been heavily dissected by gullies etched into
the volcanic soils that lie on top of older mudstones.

Navigable for much of its length, the Whanganui River nears the end of its 290 km journey from the western flanks of Mt Tongariro to the sea.

TOP: Farmland reverting to scrub in the middle reaches of the Whanganui River, where pioneer dreams have exceeded the capabilities of the land.

ABOVE: The city of Wanganui near the mouth of the river from which it takes its name.

OPPOSITE: The first tints of morning sun catch the high eastern slopes of Mt Ngauruhoe and Mt Ruapehu.

A small cloud of hot volcanic steam rises from the ice-encrusted crater of Mt Ngauruhoe. The mountain puffs out steam and gas continuously, and every few years turns on a more dramatic eruption of ash and lava.

ABOVE: Ash deposits streaked with winter snows south of
Mt Ngauruhoe.

LEFT: The more active vents of Tongariro National Park provide
a striking example of the tendency of volcanoes to erupt along a
line of weakness in the Earth's crust. In this photograph the older
vents of Te Maari Crater and Mt Tongariro's North Crater in the
foreground line up with the younger cones of Mt Ngauruhoe and
Mt Ruapehu beyond.

Mt Ruapehu cloaked in an early winter snowfall. Despite the fact that the volcano is still very active, thousands of visitors flock to the three skifields on its upper slopes each winter.

Volcanic cliffs on the western shores of Lake Taupo, where rapidly cooling ignimbrite has formed impressive regular columns.

OPPOSITE: The sacred volcanic mountains of Tongariro National Park rise beyond the southern shores of Lake Taupo.

ABOVE: Farmland on volcanic pumice soils near Lake Taupo. Initial attempts to farm these soils were thwarted by a puzzling stock malady called "bush sickness". Eventually deficiencies of cobalt, selenium and copper were identified as the cause, and the introduction of corrective fertilisers led to a rapid growth in pastoral farming in the region.

TOP LEFT: Generating electricity with geothermal energy at Wairakei, north of Lake Taupo.

LEFT: Introduced pines have been planted over vast areas of the Volcanic Plateau, many of them during the Depression of the 1930s when the region was considered unsuitable for pastoral farming (see ABOVE).

OPPOSITE: The 900-year-old explosion crater occupied by the Champagne Pool and surrounding sinter terraces at Waiotapu ("sacred waters"), south of Rotorua. The striking colours result from high concentrations of chemical elements like arsenic, antimony, sulphur, iron and gold precipitated in the seepages and stagnant pools.

A huge rift slices across the summit of Mt Tarawera. It was formed during a massive eruption in 1886 that killed more than 150 people, obliterated the magnificent Pink and White Terraces along the shores of nearby Lake Rotomahana, and increased the size of the lake about 20 times.

OPPOSITE: Smoke billows from the active main crater of White Island, off the Bay of Plenty coast.

Wahanga and Ruawahia, the two other flat-topped rhyolite lava domes that make up the Tarawera volcanic complex.

ABOVE: Winter frosts coat rich dairying land north of Taupo.

TOP LEFT: The ancient volcano of Mt Maunganui on the Bay of Plenty coastline, with the southern entrance to Tauranga Harbour and Matakana Island beyond.

LEFT: Built in 1953 as a "model" town, Kawerau services a huge pulp and paper mill that processes timber from the vast pine forests of the central North Island.

OPPOSITE : Kiwifruit orchards near Te Puke. The first commercial crop of what were then "chinese gooseberries" was planted in this area in 1934, but the fruit only really became popular when the name "kiwifruit" was introduced in the early 1970s. The resulting boom in the market saw thousands of hectares of land in the Bay of Plenty and other parts of the country converted to kiwifruit vines.

CHAPTER 8
Auckland, Coromandel & Northland

Auckland's Westhaven Marina.

OPPOSITE: The downtown area and waterfront of Auckland, New Zealand's largest city and home of nearly a third of its people.

LAND AND sea interweave in the north of New Zealand like old familiar lovers, as the sea, gradually rising since the Ice Ages, has come to engulf ancient valleys and low-lying plains. The main northern peninsula is long and narrow — 80 km between coasts at its widest, 11 km on the Auckland isthmus, and only a stone's throw across at its narrowest point. Much of the West Coast extends in long, straight expanses of beach and dune that are pounded by the relentless swells of the Tasman Sea. It is breached by three great intrusions, the flooded valley systems of the Hokianga, Kaipara and Manukau

Harbours, whose expansive inland waterways reach deeply into the land's interior.

To the east the coastline curves and twists with a more gentle and intricate anatomy, indented with numerous small bays, inlets and estuaries. Thousands of years ago, when colder climates locked much of the sea in ice, this eastern coastline would have reached out as far as Great Barrier Island, and the Coromandel Peninsula would have been joined down its length to the main northern landmass. Here, what was once land is now covered with the waters of the Firth of Thames, the Hauraki Gulf and the Bay of Islands, and only the tops of former hills and volcanoes rise from the ocean.

Most of the more recent landforms of this region have been shaped by volcanic activity that, over millions of years, has built a terrain of cones and lava flows, overlaying older sedimentary landscapes. The Far North has over 25 known eruption points, while the Auckland area is dotted with at least 50 volcanic cones. This latter volcanic field has by no means spent its energy, and eruptions only a few hundred years ago created Rangitoto Island, the symmetrical island cone that stands, sentinel-like, opposite the entrance to Auckland's Waitemata Harbour.

The north enjoys the warmest climate in New Zealand (although not the sunniest — the weather tends to be humid in summer and wet in winter) and this, along with the rich forests and abundance of fish and shellfish, attracted the first Polynesian settlers to the region. Most prominent headlands, volcanic cones and islands bear the characteristic marks of Maori habitation: terraced slopes, food storage pits and fortification ditches. Some of the bigger volcanic cones of the Auckland isthmus, such as Mt Eden, One Tree Hill and Mangere Mountain, were the centres of the largest prehistoric Polynesian communities ever to have existed. Well over 20,000 Maori are thought to have been living in the greater Auckland area of Tamaki-Makau-Rau (Land of Many Lovers) before Europeans arrived.

The north's abundance of natural resources soon attracted European colonists, who hunted the whales that migrated through its coastal waters, mined the Coromandel's rich gold deposits, and exploited the timber. Northland, which now has large areas of reverting farmland and exotic forest plantations, was once covered with forests of one of the world's most extraordinary trees, the kauri. Native to New Zealand and only found in this northern region, the kauri grows with a tall, fat, branchless trunk and a high crown of foliage. It soon gained a reputation both as the world's biggest timber tree and as the best for boat building, and by the 1850s kauri was New Zealand's most important export. Sadly, 150 years of milling has left only remnants of kauri forest, now protected in small sanctuaries in Northland and Coromandel, with the largest tree, Tane Mahuta (51 m high, over 1200 years old and with a girth of 14 m), testimony to the giants that once populated this whole area.

The north remains the most densely settled region in New Zealand. Auckland alone has almost one third of New Zealand's total population, well in excess of the entire population of the South Island. Over 10% of the city's inhabitants are Polynesian — Maori and a mix of other Pacific Island cultures — making Auckland the largest Polynesian city in the world. It is the country's commercial centre, principal port and main point of entry and exit for overseas travellers. Urban development sprawls over some 5200 km², and includes nine separate cities, all under the umbrella of the Auckland metropolis. The central business area is highrise, glassy and glossy, and Auckland's many suburbs reflect a wide spectrum of styles, culture and wealth.

East of Auckland lie the Hauraki Gulf and the Coromandel Peninsula, both used extensively by Aucklanders for escape and recreation. They also have a very important role in preserving the natural values of this most populous part of the country. This is especially true of some of the islands of the Hauraki Gulf and Bay of Islands Maritime Parks, which, largely free of introduced predators and browsing animals, have assumed international significance as sanctuaries for endangered wildlife and plants.

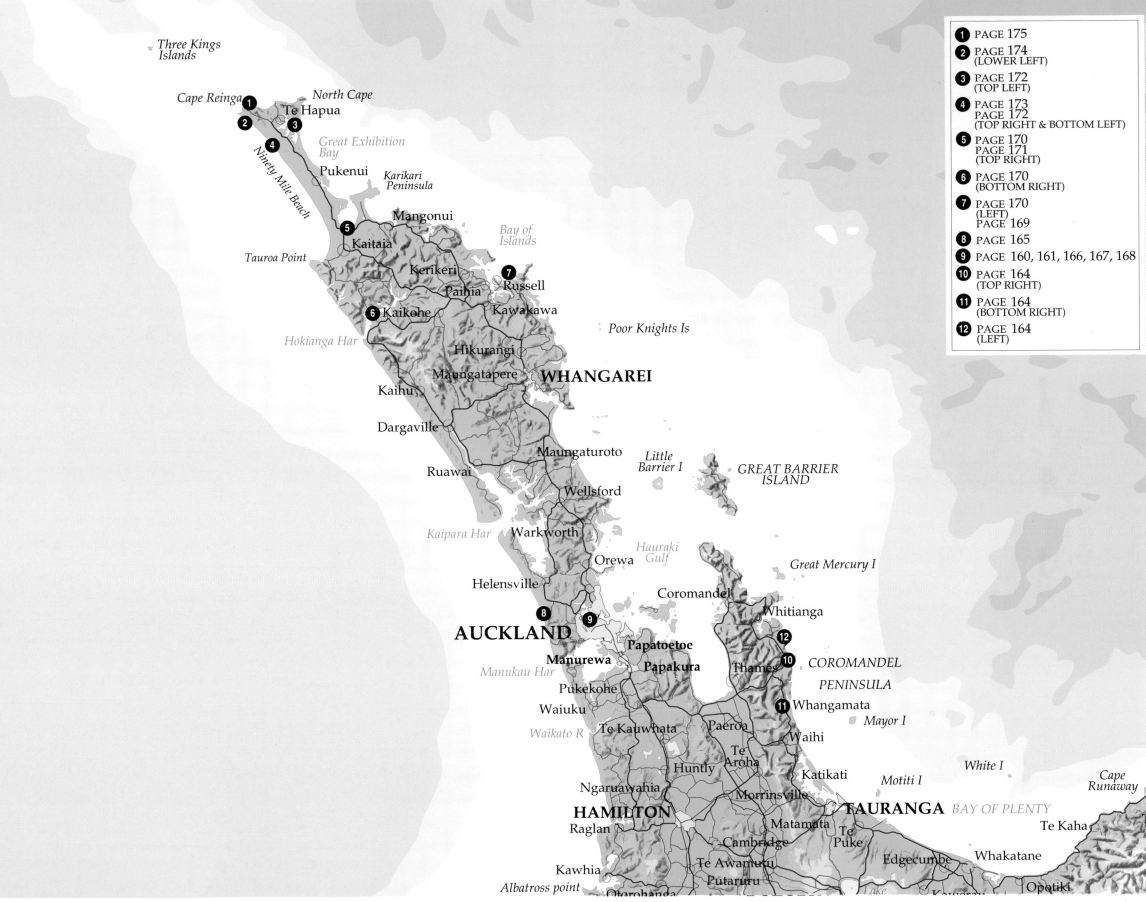

Three Kings
Islands

Cape Reinga ① North Cape
② Te Hapua
③
Great Exhibition
④ Bay
Pukenui Karikari
Peninsula

Ninety Mile Beach

Mangonui

⑤ Kaitaia Bay of
Islands
Tauroa Point
Kerikeri
Paihia ⑦ Russell
⑥ Kaikohe Kawakawa

Hokianga Har Poor Knights Is

Hikurangi

Maungatapere WHANGAREI

Kaihu

Dargaville

Maungaturoto Little
Barrier I GREAT BARRIER
ISLAND
Ruawai

Wellsford

Kaipara Har Warkworth

Orewa Hauraki
Gulf Great Mercury I

Helensville

Coromandel
Whitianga
⑧ AUCKLAND ⑨ ⑫
Papatoetoe
Manukau Har Manurewa Thames ⑩ COROMANDEL
Papakura
PENINSULA
Pukekohe
Waiuku ⑪ Whangamata
Waikato R Te Kauwhata Paeroa Mayor I
Waihi
Te
Huntly Aroha
Katikati White I
Ngaruawahia Motiti I Cape
Morrinsville Runaway
HAMILTON TAURANGA BAY OF PLENTY
Raglan Matamata Te
Puke Te Kaha
Cambridge Edgecumbe
Kawhia Te Awamutu Whakatane
Albatross point Putaruru Opotiki
Otorohanga

Less than two hours' drive from Auckland or Hamilton, the Coromandel Peninsula's many beautiful beaches provide ideal retreats from busy city life. ABOVE: Precipitous cliffs at Mercury Bay.
TOP RIGHT: Sandy coves near Pauanui.
BOTTOM RIGHT: The seaside resort of Whangamata.

OPPOSITE: Gannets find a safe nesting retreat amidst turbulent seas on the flat top of Gannet Rock, off Muriwai on Auckland's exposed West Coast.

Office blocks in downtown Auckland early on a winter's evening.

Auckland's Harbour Bridge spans the Waitemata Harbour, linking central parts of the city with its extensive North Shore suburbs.

Auckland's North-western Motorway helps to make connections in this expansive city whose suburbs sprawl over a wide area indented by many harbours, bays and estuaries.

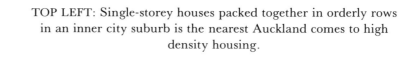
ABOVE: Swimming pool at Auckland's Regent Hotel.

TOP LEFT: Single-storey houses packed together in orderly rows in an inner city suburb is the nearest Auckland comes to high density housing.

LEFT: The summit of Maungakiekie or One Tree Hill (195 m), the highest of the volcanic cones in the Auckland City area.

OPPOSITE: The clear turquoise waters and curving white sands of Motuarohia (Roberton Island) in the Bay of Islands attract many visitors. The middle part of the island is a recreation reserve, with a popular underwater trail in the outer lagoon.

The Black Rocks off Moturoa Island in the Bay of Islands, spectacular jointed columns of volcanic rock whose sides drop sheer to the sea floor.

TOP: Sinuous curves in the Awanui River as it flows through fields and mangroves into Northland's Rangaunu Harbour. ABOVE: Upper reaches of the Hokianga Harbour, a system of old river valleys invaded by the sea on the west coast of Northland.

Mangroves growing in the muddy and salty environment of Northland's Rangaunu Harbour. Found only in the northern regions of New Zealand, mangrove trees can tolerate long periods of immersion in salt water, and are important breeding and feeding grounds for many coastal fish.

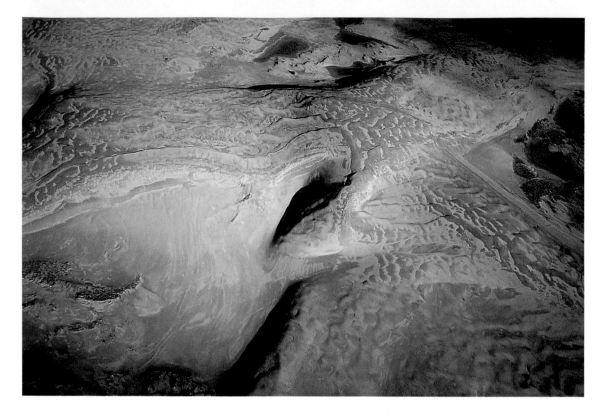

TOP LEFT: Parengarenga Harbour, near North Cape. In early March the harbour is the gathering point from which godwits set off on their long flight "home" to Siberia and Alaska after migrating to New Zealand to escape the northern winter.

ABOVE & LOWER LEFT: The Te Paki Coastal Park protects 23,000 hectares of coastline, dunes, wetlands and forests at the top of New Zealand, including parts of Ninety Mile Beach. Along the western side of the park westerly winds have sculpted huge sand dunes up to 100 m high, which form dramatic boundaries with the adjoining pasture and forest.

OPPOSITE: Looking south down Ninety Mile Beach, a great expanse of windblown sands that makes up the northernmost segment of the North Island's west coast.

Sands pile up against the clays of older marine sediments near the
northern end of Ninety Mile Beach.

ABOVE: The derelict lighthouse at Cape Maria van Diemen at the northern end of Ninety Mile Beach. The cape was named in 1642 by the Dutch navigator Abel Tasman, one of only two names given by Tasman to features on the New Zealand coast that still appear on our maps today. (The other is the Three Kings Islands.)

RIGHT: Cape Reinga, at the northwestern tip of New Zealand, is one of the most sacred Maori places in the country. From here the spirits of the dead take their final departure from Aotearoa, descending to the lone pohutukawa tree that clings to the edge of the headland and from there leaping into the ocean.
(Reinga means "place of leaping".)